I0605085

Praise for How Joyous Effort Works

"Janet Ettele's books are part of a cultural renaissance which brings European and American forms more deeply into dialogue and interaction with Buddhist inner sciences, philosophy, psychology and practice than ever before. The tradition of bringing insights, practices and philosophy from Buddhism into the form of the novel began with writers like J.D. Salinger and Jack Keroac, and Janet continues that cross-cultural exploration in a way that reflects deep curiosity and kindness. In a culture that's too often addicted to meaningless drama, Janet gives us a grounded story with characters who reflect deeply as they explore the authentic questions of how to live wisely with compassion and joyous efforts."

—Lorne Ladner, PhD, Author of *The Lost Art of Compassion*

"How Joyous Effort Works by Janet Ettele offers step by step advice on how to cultivate enthusiastic joy for developing positive inner states like equanimity, gratitude, patience, concentration, and wisdom. Janet imparts these insights within the context of a heart-warming story of a young man, Troy, seeking guidance and meaningful relationships. This book is an invaluable resource for anyone who wishes to live a meaningful life."

—Wilson Hurley, Therapist, Teacher, Author:
Compassion's COMPASS: Strategies for Developing Insight, Kindness, and Empathy

"*How Joyous Effort Works* is pure and optimistic, with a magnetism that won't quit. Janet Ettele has created archetypal characters, with one foot in this world and one beyond; I couldn't put it down."

—Dr. David Kittay, Columbia University
Department of Religion; Translator of The Vajra
Rosary Tantra and The Dharma Council Sutra

"Ms. Ettele integrates complex Buddhist teachings in a simple yet powerful way that keeps the reader engaged and connected to Buddhism."

—Paul Neri, Luthier, and Author
of the Acoustic Guitar Repair Detective

How Joyous Effort Works

The Energy to Benefit Others

Janet Kathleen Ettele

Book design by Clare Cerullo

Printed in the United States of America

Library of Congress Cataloging-in-Publication Data is available upon request.

ISBN 9781939839060

For more information about the How Life Works series and the author, please visit www.janetettele.com.

Dedicated to the great teacher, Master Shantideva, whose precious teaching of the Bodhicaryavatara continues to illuminate the Buddha's path for the benefit of all sentient beings.

THE DALAI LAMA

FOREWORD

The Buddha came to this world around 2600 years ago and gave his teachings in India. The universality of his teachings is evidenced by the fact that many people throughout the modern world find them beneficial in many ways. Certainly, his extensive teachings on altruism and the concept of dependent origination are not merely with a spiritual basis but their benefits are validated by science.

Obviously, it goes without saying that one has to have a proper understanding of the teachings to avail oneself of its benefits. This includes training of one's mind. The nature of our human thoughts and emotions are such that the more you develop them, the more powerful they become.

Janet Kathleen Ettele's "How Joyous Efforts Work" introduces Buddhism interweaving it with stories of our daily life. I hope this book enables the general readers to get a better understanding of the Buddhist teachings, getting conviction not because of faith, but due to reasoning.

22 November 2022

Introduction

A Guide to the Bodhisattva's Way of Life (Bodhichayavatara) was first taught by Master Shantideva in India during the eighth century. He was born a prince, but chose the life of a monk and studied at Nalanda University. While at Nalanda, Master Shantideva appeared to do nothing but sleep, eat, and other necessary functions of the body and was perceived by the other monks to be an embarrassment to their prestigious university. The monks resented him for his laziness, and since there were rules that prevented them from having him expelled, they designed a plan they believed would be a perfect way to shame him into voluntarily leaving Nalanda. The plan included ordering him to give a public teaching. They thought that certainly he would realize that since he knew nothing and had nothing of value to teach, he would run away to avoid humiliation.

In the center of a field, they prepared a very high throne for him to teach from and invited people from all the surrounding areas to attend. To increase the challenge, they asked him to teach something that had never been taught before. Determined to leave no stone unturned in their effort to humiliate him, they had built the throne with no stairs by which to reach its seat. When Shantideva approached the throne, he placed his hand on its side and was immediately transported to the seat of the throne. Then, Shantideva proceeded to speak eloquently and spontaneously, reciting the Bodhichayavatara, which is now one of the most renowned texts in Buddhism. To the astonishment of those in attendance, the profound teaching flowed from Shantideva in the form of song-like poetry. It has been said that when Master Shantideva reached the final chapter on the Perfection of Wisdom, that his body raised higher and higher from the seat of the throne until he eventually disappeared from sight. His teaching continued but was only heard by those who having attained higher realizations in their own minds had the ability to hear.

A Guide to the Bodhisattva's Way of Life has provided students of the Buddhist Dharma from that day forward with a clear and wisdom filled path on how to practice what is commonly known as the Six Paramitas, or the Six Perfections. The Six Perfections provide the necessary guidance on how a Bodhisattva, motivated by compassion and the intention to benefit all beings, must perfect his or her mind on the path to enlightenment. For ordinary people like most of us, the verses provide the perfect guidance to live happy and meaningful lives.

How Joyous Efforts Work is based on the fourth Perfection of Master Shantideva's *Guide to the Bodhisattva's Way of Life*—the Perfection of Joyous Effort. This has also been translated as Joyful Effort, Joyful Diligence, Endeavor, Vigor, Enthusiasm, or Perseverance. The Sanskrit name for this Perfection is *Virya* which, among many other meanings in English, is Energy. So, we get the idea that no matter what you call it, a great deal of effort and energy is required. But what about the joyful and enthusiastic part? When there's something we are intent on doing, our determination gives us energy to pursue the accomplishment of whatever that is. And when we have the sense that the result of our pursuit will be one that brings about a truly beneficial outcome such as happiness and peace, then our efforts will be fueled with the additional energy of joy. With confidence that the goal of our aspiration is achievable we don't give up when things are hard or inconvenient, but we will take setbacks in stride, and even take time to rest and recharge when needed.

The passages from Shantideva's teachings included in this book are as written in *A Guide to the*

Bodhisattva's Way of Life, Translated by Stephen Batchelor from the Library of Tibetan Works and Archives, Dharmsala.

Just as the wind blowing back and forth
Controls (the movement of) a piece of cotton,
So shall I be controlled by joy,
And in this way accomplish everything.
VII. 76

There's something sacred about rivers—the way they carry life within them like a mother carries her children in her heart, all breathing the same loving essence no matter how distant they flow. This thought and others ran through Troy's mind as he drove, following the river to Abe's shop. The view had changed since the last time he'd been on this road. Layers of dense green leaves now screened the water that had grown shallow, and the water moved much more slowly than it had during the rushing from April's snow melt. July heat slows all kinds of things; everything except tomatoes, snap beans, or blackberries that tangle their way through gardens like there's no tomorrow, and the night sounds are vibrant when the warm and gentle light of the moon and stars draw the nocturnal from their daytime slumber.

Troy turned off the music he had been listening to as he approached the river. Intently focused on the purpose of his trip, there was no space for distraction.

When he'd called Abe the day before, the months since they'd last been in touch vanished into a conversation that was brief and to the point: "Come tomorrow morning," Abe said. "We'll talk then."

Troy's spring semester had ended a few weeks earlier, and now he was following through on his commitment to spend the summer going more deeply into dharma study. Although the word *Dharma* has many meanings, mostly coming from India, it is a word that had become part of his vocabulary beginning only seven months earlier when he crossed paths with Buddhist teachings and came to understand it to represent the teachings as a whole. It was a time when he had hit rock bottom in his life, but then things began to change when he met some wise and generous people, each of whom offered guidance and help. Abe was one of them.

Troy turned into the unpaved lot, the crunch of sand and gravel under his tires a welcoming sound. He turned off the engine and left the truck in gear. Taking the orange book Mrs. Sternau had given him along with the container of brownies that Maggie had made, he walked into the familiar musty smell of Abe's shop. Troy looked around, curious to see what new pieces had been added to the inventory since the last time he had been there. An antique prism threw shimmering patches of rainbows onto the wall, and on his way to the staircase that led to Abe's apartment he passed a pair of Victorian chairs with red velvet upholstery, nesting tables with carved trim, and an oval table of white marble on a dark wood base. It felt like coming home.

Abe opened the door before Troy reached the top of the stairs. "Hey, buddy, glad to see you—come on in."

"These are from Maggie," Troy said, handing him the brownies.

"Ah, she knows my favorite weakness! Thanks." Abe led the way into the kitchen and placed them on the table. "How about some coffee or tea to go with the brownies?"

"Coffee sounds good." Troy put his book on the table and stepped closer to the window that overlooked the road. The river was barely visible now through the dense foliage of the trees.

"Have a seat," Abe said, handing a mug of steaming coffee to Troy. "Cream or sugar?"

"Neither, thank you."

Abe joined Troy at the table with his coffee, and lifted a brownie from the container. "So, tell me about the elderly woman you mentioned when you called."

"Her name is Mrs. Sternau. Among other things, she taught me about the power that comes from the practice of patience. And through that practice I was able to begin transforming my relationship with my stepmother, Maureen. It was a milestone, actually, because ever since my father married Maureen, I felt she's had it in for me. Mrs. Sternau guided me through a horrible situation that came up between Maureen and me. I decided to pour everything I'd learned from her into resolving it. The outcome was better than I could have imagined." He laughed, "Maureen actually apologized, and even asked for my help to change the way she behaves."

"You said this woman, Mrs. Sternau, gave you a book on the dharma and that you want to talk to me about studying more." He nodded toward the orange book. "But, if it's that book you want to study, why aren't you asking her to help you?"

"Well, it's not just the book she gave me that I want to study. I want to study everything. I just don't know where to start. You and I have talked openly about our pasts; you get where I'm coming from and, well, there are just some things I'm more comfortable talking about with you."

Abe broke off a piece of brownie and popped it into his mouth. "I'm always happy to talk about the dharma. In my opinion, it's the most worthwhile conversation to have." He dunked the last corner of his brownie into his coffee. "Think of the path of the dharma as circular—you can step into it at any place, wherever you need, or for a lot of people, wherever you land. Having said that, the best way to learn is under the guidance of a teacher with certain important qualities. By this I mean someone who has mastered all the dharma teachings, and most importantly practices them. And for the record, I don't come close to fitting that description. The teacher I'm describing isn't always someone making a big splash in the world or claiming to have superior powers or attainments. Very often, the real deal is someone who might appear to be very humble. You'll only come to recognize a teacher's qualities as you continue to study and practice, and by observing him or her over time. In fact, in sacred writings and commentaries it's advised to observe a teacher for twelve years before accepting him or her as your teacher. These days, people don't like to wait that long. Maybe they don't feel they have the time; I don't really know the reason people are in such a hurry. In my opinion, when it comes to something as important as attaining the level of trust you need in whom you choose as your dharma teacher, it's not going to happen overnight. A qualified teacher is extremely rare to find, and if you were to find one you would make every effort to stay close to him or her and take in everything you could. I found that quality in Rinpoche, the teacher I told you about last spring. He passed away over fifteen years ago. He was an extraordinary teacher. While I'm glad to help you in any way I can, I know enough to know that I am limited in what I can offer.

"I have an idea though." Abe wiped the crumbs from the table with the side of his hand and brushed them onto his plate. "I want to introduce you to someone I have the highest respect for. In fact, he's the guy I brought your guitar to last spring when I had it polished and restrung for you. He's a luthier, a master of his craft, and also a devoted practitioner of the dharma. He was a student of Rinpoche's too—that's how we met each other. He lives only about ten miles from here." Abe lifted the plate of brownies, "Do you want any more of these?"

"No thanks."

"I've got to put them away—I have no restraint when it comes to chocolate!" Abe carried the brownies to the counter, sealed the cover over them, and gazed out the window for a moment before turning back to Troy. "My friend's name is Julian, and the more I think about it, the more convinced I am that you two should meet."

"Abe, you're definitely being humble. You've already taught me so much that's helped me tremendously, and I can't thank you enough. But if you think I should study with Julian then I trust you, and I'd absolutely love to meet him. The sooner the better. That is, if he's not too busy."

"Jules is really selective about how he spends his time. If you get to know him, you'll see that in his own very quiet way, no matter what he's doing, he's always practicing the dharma. And if that's what you're interested in doing too—which it sounds like you are—then he'll have all the time in the world."

"So, when can I meet him?" Troy asked.

"I'll call him tonight. I'll be in touch with you as soon as I've talked to him, but the thing with Jules is that I never know what he's got going on. He makes silent retreats a part of his dharma practice, and whenever he's doing one, he's just not reachable.

"In the meantime, if you're going to dedicate a chunk of effort to studying and practicing dharma, and you want good results, spend some time thinking about your motivation for wanting to engage in the dharma. A lot of people tend to forget about this fundamental factor when they embark on the path of practicing dharma, and, in that case, years can go by without having made much progress. So, think carefully about whatever it is you're after. What's your purpose in studying and practicing? Your motivation will be the thing that guides you and supports your determination when you hit the inevitable bumps in the road. Think about it. People study medicine for all kinds of reasons, right? If you want to become a doctor, you're looking at years and years of hard work—and not all of it is pleasant. Not everyone in medical school has the same motivation, but whatever the motivation is, it becomes the fuel that keeps them going when challenges are their most extreme. In the case of dharma study and practice, if you fully understand why it's a worthwhile endeavor, your effort will be joyful. Rinpoche used to tell us that joyous effort is like the wind that pushes you toward your goal."

"I don't know that I even have a goal, Abe. I mean, right now I'm just really intrigued by what I've learned and how much things in my life have changed. I think that's mostly because I've learned to think about and react to things differently, and therefore I've handled things differently. The more I've begun to understand and experience events differently in my life due to dharma study and practice, the more I feel my life is worth living. I haven't said this to anyone before, but there were a lot of times in the last few years when I honestly didn't care if I lived or died. And, it didn't seem like anyone else cared either." Troy watched clouds of dust float in a beam of light that poured through the open window. He cleared the tightness from his throat, "I see things from a different perspective now, and the memory of that experience feels distant. I mean, I can remember it and tell you about it, but the overwhelming sense of despair I used to feel has changed, and it's like some of the things that I used to be so bummed out about or that I used to fear no longer have any power over me."

"I'm not surprised to hear you say that," Abe said. "The dharma has that effect of transforming experiences of suffering into something that can be experienced as joyful, even the intense experiences like you're describing.

"So, let's talk about The Four Noble Truths, Buddha's first teaching. It sounds pretty simple; like there are only four things you need to know, right? On the surface, it's simple and, once understood, it's simple again. But getting from the surface to the fullest understanding takes some serious study, contemplation, and meditation. Yet, it's so relevant to every aspect of daily life that I wish people would make an effort to understand it, whether they have an inclination toward a spiritual path or not."

"The Four Noble Truths—that's what the friend you served with in Vietnam talked about." Troy recalled the morning Abe told him about his own introduction to the dharma back in the 1960s.

"Yeah, that was Eddie." Abe shook his head, "I still miss that guy. What a brave and crazy soul he was."

"I love the picture you have in your office—the one of you, Eddie, and the other guys you served with. How did you all manage to look so relaxed in the middle of a war?"

"We were far from relaxed!" Abe laughed. "What you see in that picture is fear hiding behind the mask of youthful defiance. Our lives depended on that defiance, and even though Eddie had it in spades, it didn't save him from the bullets that killed him.

"But getting back to the Four Noble Truths. You can work with them in your meditation practice while you're waiting to meet Jules. The first is the truth of suffering. We know there's suffering on an obvious level. In Buddhism it is called the 'suffering of suffering.' It's in our faces constantly: the pain of birth, old age, sickness, and death, as the Buddha described it. But you need to be aware of the subtle levels of suffering that we come to understand as we deepen our study and practice. The purpose is not to make you miserable, but to help you avoid setting yourself up for more, and actually transform suffering into joy. Remember, the word 'suffering' is used really broadly here. As in the 'suffering of suffering,' it includes intense and painful suffering, but it also describes the petty things that people can get all worked up over. There's suffering that comes as a result of change like, on a big scale, when someone we are very close to dies, or on a smaller scale, when an object you're really fond of breaks. It's the inevitable experience of change that comes when something that was once a source of pleasure no longer can possibly be pleasurable, and so it becomes a source of pain. In Buddhism this is called the 'suffering of change.' Then, there are even more subtle levels of suffering that we experience because we haven't learned to recognize their presence. In Buddhism, these subtle levels of suffering are called 'pervasive suffering' and are so interwoven into existence they're just sort of humming along. It's the general background of anxiety and insecurity that colors even our happiest moments. Deep down, we fear that life doesn't offer us solid ground and that our very existence is questionable.

From a Buddhist point of view, these doubts are well-founded, and exploring them offers us glimpses of wisdom. And as we learn to recognize them, they can become very instructive in our practice, leading to the transformation of suffering into joy and happiness.

"The second noble truth states that there are causes of suffering. Specifically, the origins of suffering within our own minds that cause suffering. There are obvious causes of the 'suffering of suffering' which we can observe and learn from and which then can help guide our understanding of the subtle causes of the 'suffering of change' and 'pervasive suffering.'

"The third noble truth is the 'truth of cessation,' meaning that because the causes of suffering originate within our own minds, we can learn to understand what these causes are, and then take certain actions to end them.

"The fourth noble truth is the 'truth of the path,' meaning that there is a method, or path, to accomplish the cessation of suffering. What is this path? It's engaging in daily practices that are based on the dharma. Through effort made doing these practices, we lay the foundation to develop wisdom, which is the main factor in eliminating the causes and conditions for suffering.

"So, knowing these Four Noble Truths is the basis of developing confidence in what they teach, and that leads to conviction and enthusiasm to practice the dharma. This conviction brings genuine joy in making the effort to create this path for oneself and for others; the actual means of ending the cycle of suffering existence."

"I've heard you mention a name for that cycle, Abe, but I forget what it's called."

"Oh, you're thinking of *samsara*, or *cyclic existence*."

"That's it. It's the cycle of things we do over and over again and that we're drawn to, like moths to a flame, right? Similar to the way we're all blindly attracted to things that end up causing us more harm than good. We think something's going to make us happy and content even though the thing itself has absolutely no quality of its own to deliver happiness…at least not the kind of happiness that can last, or that won't later turn into something disappointing or even painful."

"You've got the idea. I think the thing that's good to keep in mind when studying dharma, and probably studying anything for that matter, is that there are always deeper levels to everything. So, the Four Noble Truths, and anything else you'll come across in studying the dharma, will only make sense to the extent you put effort into gaining knowledge and reflecting on what you learn. That's when it really becomes a part of how you approach and truly understand life, and the reflection aspect is one of the many reasons why meditation is so important. It's not enough to only listen to someone teach or to just read a book, because until you've integrated knowledge as your own, its power to help you is only minimal."

"I meditate every day now, Abe, but sometimes I just sit there chasing my mind—or maybe it's my mind that's chasing me—it's hard to know the difference. I try following my breath, counting each breath coming in and going out so I can train my mind to focus. There are times when I do pretty well and I feel I'm making progress, but other times I feel like my effort is a waste of time."

"Never consider your effort a waste of time. Nothing happens without effort, and if you think that anything worthwhile has ever manifested without a mixture of success and setbacks, you're not seeing the whole picture.

"The intangible nature of the mind makes it difficult for people to recognize that just like the body, the mind also needs discipline and training if it's going to develop into its potential. Marathon runners don't question the value of the effort they pour into training their bodies: watching what they eat, pushing themselves through physical and mental discomfort, taking care of their injuries, learning how to prevent injuries, all so they can increase their endurance and speed and do their absolute best. Why would we approach training our minds any differently? First you have to know the importance of training the mind. I suppose it's because we can't see the mind that many people don't even think about it and have no clue where their minds are half the time. The nature of an untrained mind is one of distraction. Since the lives we lead are a manifestation of the quality of our mind, it's no wonder so many people feel their lives are out of control."

"You're right. I guess any effort in that direction is worthwhile. It's just that there are times when I get really frustrated, that's all."

"Discouragement is a big obstacle, Troy. Don't worry; you'll learn how to counteract that one by turning even that into the path. For now, just keep up with what you've been doing and bring the Four Noble Truths into your meditation practice. In time, your motivation and purpose will become clear."

"Sounds good. I can do that." Troy checked the time on the clock on the wall. "I guess I ought to get going. You've probably got stuff to do, and I told my mom I'd stop by to see her before I head into work this afternoon."

"Good to see you, Troy. Thanks for coming by. I'll get in touch with Jules, and I'll let you know as soon as I reach him."

As Troy made his way toward the staircase to leave, Abe said, "I almost forgot, I have something for you to give Maggie. I'll walk out with you." Troy followed Abe down the stairs, noticing what looked like the same spider he had seen spinning its web in the window near the jade plant only a few months earlier. The hot, humid air that came through the open window intensified the musty scent of antique wood, and the stairs moaned wearily under the weight of their footsteps.

"Here's an easel that just came in the other day. I know she already has one, but I thought Maggie could use another. The legs telescope in so she can easily fold the thing up and put it in her car and take it anywhere she wants." Abe demonstrated how to open the easel and then folded it up again and handed it to Troy.

"She'll love it. Thanks. I'll give it to her later today when I see her." The two walked together outside, and Troy leaned the easel against his truck while he fished his keys from his jeans' pocket. "And thanks for helping to put me in touch with your friend. I hope it'll work out."

"It will," Abe said. "I'll get back to you real soon."

~

The drive to his mother's passed quickly. Troy's mind raced with excitement from his conversation with Abe. Pulling into the apartment complex, he looked for a place in the shade to park, and found a spot behind the brick building by one of the maples near the asphalt lot.

Troy climbed the flight of stairs that ran along the side of the building, and turned down the corridor that led to his mother's door.

Troy knocked loudly on the door. "Mom?" A strip of paper printed with the words "out of order" was taped over the doorbell. It had been there for months.

"Hi, honey!" Troy thought his mother looked small standing in the doorway, smaller, at least, than the image he held of her in his mind. They exchanged hugs and Troy kicked his sandals off to leave them by the door.

"Would you like something cold to drink?" she asked. She pulled her long hair up off her neck and fastened it lopsidedly with a clip. Troy noticed strands of white were becoming more prominent within her auburn hair.

"Sure, what've you got?" He followed her into the kitchen.

"Let's see," she opened the refrigerator, "I've got iced tea, orange juice, pomegranate juice—that's really good for you, you know, and it's fabulous mixed with seltzer water." She pushed things around on the shelves to get a better look, "Um, well I guess that's about it."

"I'll try the pomegranate juice with seltzer."

She poured the juice and seltzer into a glass with ice and handed it to Troy.

"So, I've got some news," she announced as she put the bottles back in the fridge and wiped the counter.

"What's up?" Troy positioned himself to stand in the breeze from the fan between the kitchen and the living room. It was actually one large room divided by a dingy brass strip where the dull sage carpet met the grey linoleum of the kitchen floor.

"Well, two things—no, actually it might be three things." She turned to face Troy, smiling while tears moistened her dark brown eyes. "They've promoted me from receptionist to office manager at the nursing home. That means I'll have more responsibilities, but I'll also be paid more money."

"That's great, Mom. Congratulations!"

"So, there's more." She handed Troy a letter that had been on the counter, the paper still creased in thirds, "Here, read this; it's from Uncle Jonathan."

Dear Rita,

Although distance has made it difficult for us to see each other, I want you to know that you've always remained close in our hearts. Francesca and I have always loved you and considered you part of our family. Before she died, we both agreed that we would like to leave you with a little something. While we don't have a significant fortune, we have enough to share, and knowing how difficult things have been for you since Brian left your marriage, we both have wished we could do something to help. I hope the enclosed will help lift your spirits and make life just a little easier for you.

With much love,
Jonathan

When she saw Troy had finished reading, she handed him the check that had come with the letter.

"Ten thousand dollars? Holy shit! Uh, sorry, Mom, but can Uncle Jonathan really afford it? I mean, he's pretty old, doesn't he need to hold onto his money in case he gets seriously ill or something?" Troy studied the unsteady handwriting that had written his mother's name in jagged script on the face of the check, and sensed the unavoidable implications that his uncle was preparing for the end of his own life. He handed the check back to his mother. "Have you talked to him about this yet?"

"I had all the same concerns you have, and yes, I have talked to him."

"Is he still living in Pennsylvania?"

"Yup. He's in the same little stone house, believe it or not. He has some neighbors who check in on him, and he's hired a housekeeper to help him with things."

Troy leaned against the counter next to his mother and put his arm around her shoulders, "If you'd like to go visit him, I'd be up for going with you. You know how I love road trips, and you and I haven't taken a trip together for years."

"I'd like that," she said. "In fact, I'd like that a lot. Thanks for offering." She wiped tears from the corners of her eyes. "I don't like driving alone at night, but if you go with me then we could drive down on a Friday night and have the weekend with him."

"Let's do it," he said. "I'll just need to talk to Theo about lining up a weekend off from work."

"Okay. So, here's the third thing. Between the raise I'm getting at work, the alimony from Dad, and this money from Uncle Jon, I can afford to move out of this apartment. I've been looking at places and found a little cottage for rent that I think could work out really well. There's space for me to set up my sewing again, and, if you want, there's a room for you too. It's small, but it has its own entrance from a little porch on the side of the house, so you could come in and out whenever. It's not nearly as big or fancy as Dad's house, but I know living with Maureen has been really uncomfortable, so I thought you might like another option while you're finishing school and getting on your feet."

"Maureen and I had what you might call a 'breakthrough' a month or so ago, Mom, and she's really trying to be nicer. Dad told me that she's begun working with a therapist. Still, I think we'd both be better off not living under the same roof." He looked out the front window of the apartment to the view of telephone lines and the back of the old lumberyard. After their divorce, moving here from the house where she and Brian had raised their family had been a rough transition for Rita. "I could help you with the rent, Mom."

"No, Troy, you've got those student loans to pay off. That's got to be your priority. I can manage. There will be plenty of things you can help me with though, so don't worry, it'll work out."

"Natalie will be upset if I leave," he winced with the thought. Natalie was only eight years old and had no understanding of their father's first marriage or her own mother's role in the intricacies of its unraveling.

"Well, you can bring her over. That is, if Maureen would allow it." She looked at Troy, "I guess that's not likely though, is it?"

"Nah," Troy laughed, "not likely. She hasn't changed that much, Mom, but maybe in time." When it came to reminders of Brian's previous marriage, most especially Troy, Maureen's reflex was to lash out over anything that rubbed her the wrong way. She treated Troy and his family as if it were they who had trespassed into her life instead of the other way around.

"The landlords seem nice enough. I've only met them once, but they said if I give them a deposit by next Friday then the place is mine." She pointed to some boxes she had stacked in the corner by the couch. "I've already begun packing. No matter what, I'm definitely getting out of here. I'd like to be out by the end of next month."

"I'll help you move, Mom. I'll see if Kyle can help too. He's got a truck, and I think that as long as you feed him, he'll be happy to help."

"That would be great. But I'll rent a van anyway, I want to do this in the fewest number of trips possible."

Troy looked around the living room and kitchen, assessing how much there was to move and then walked down the short hall to his mom's bedroom. "Mom, you don't have that much stuff here."

"I still have some furniture and boxes in storage of things that I've saved for you and your brothers. I'd love it if I could fit everything in the new place so I don't have to keep paying for storage."

"Well, if it turns out you need furniture, we can go up to Abe's place and see what he's got. Besides, I really want you to meet him."

"Let's wait 'til after I get settled in. I'll have a better idea what I might need by then. Hey, do you want to take a ride over to see the place?"

"Um, I'm sorry, I can't now. I've gotta get to work. I told Theo I'd come work the afternoon shift. The guy he has scheduled has to leave early. How about Saturday morning?"

"Sure, give me a call when you're free. I'll be spending the day packing."

"Sounds good. I better run." He hugged her, and said what he always said every time he said goodbye to her, "Love you, Mom."

"I love you too, honey. See you Saturday."

~

Relying upon the boat of a human (body),
Free yourself from the great river of pain!
As it is hard to find this boat again,
This is no time for sleep, you fool.
VII. 14

Troy felt he was on the cusp of significant change in his life and could feel the rush of its energy. But he knew the risks of getting swept away by the excitement of anticipation. The excitement was actually a good object for him to be aware of through the lens of the suffering of change. So, Troy took a moment to remember and reflect on the conversation he had earlier with Abe about the Buddha's first noble truth, in particular, the suffering of change. He thought, without a certain kind of vigilance of thought, anticipation can influence the mind with things that have no basis in reality. Conditions are always changing and by keeping that in mind one is protected from the pain of getting attached to specific outcomes. Otherwise, when things change, as they inevitably will, the result is a very painful tearing away from whatever it is one has become attached to. The nature of change has its upsides. When things are painful and challenging, one can guard against discouragement by remembering the certainty of change and therefore, it is only logical that the experience of pain will change as well.

Troy had been learning that everything he experiences is the result of previous causes, or *karma*. Seeing that there are so many moving parts at work through all his thoughts, words, and actions, and because none of these experiences are truly permanent or fixed, Troy was beginning to see his potential to transform them by creating the appropriate causes and conditions for whatever he wanted to create. A small glimpse of the experience of wisdom was starting to occur, and the joyous effort Abe talked about was something he could actually feel.

Troy understood that cause and effect is an undeniable reality, and had begun to observe some benefits that had come from mindfully creating positive causes through his actions of mind, body, and speech. Abe called these benefits "merit and virtue," that directly lead to cessation through gaining wisdom. Troy wanted to continue making effort to create the kind of causes that would ripen into positive future results, and to stop creating the causes that he knew from personal experience produce negative results. To successfully do this would require that he train his mind to be mindful and vigilant by receiving proper instruction from qualified teachers. Although he would never have predicted this a year earlier, he was on a path.

~

Maggie was already at the diner working by the time Troy arrived. He looked at the easel resting against the dashboard and wished he had a bow or something to make it look more like a gift.

Parked behind the diner, he searched through the clutter in his truck and used one of the socks he had left on his seat to wipe the dust from the wood, carefully removing the sand and dirt that had collected near the hinges. "It'll have to do," he muttered to himself as he tossed the sock back onto the seat and headed into work.

He walked through the back entrance to the kitchen where Theo was slicing thick sandwiches held together with cellophane fringed toothpicks arranged on plates with pickles, chips, and coleslaw.

"Hey, Troy, glad to see you," he said.

"Hey, Theo, how's it goin'?"

"Not bad," he said. "How's the heat out there?"

"Hot as hell."

Maggie came into the kitchen carrying a tray. "Hey, hon!" she smiled at Troy and brushed him with a kiss on her way to pick up the orders from Theo.

"Theo, I need another order of fries, please." Carrying the full tray back to the dining area, she turned toward Troy, "How's Abe? Did he like the brownies?"

"He loved them," Troy answered.

And there was her smile; the smile he could never get enough of.

Troy left the kitchen to find Alex and let him know he'd arrived.

"You got here just in time," Alex said, carrying a bus pan filled with dishes and silverware to the kitchen.

"Thanks for covering for me—I owe you one," he said on his way out.

"No problem."

"I've gotta fly. See you next week."

"See ya," Troy said, looking around to see what needed doing. A young couple was leaving a table in the far corner. Troy grabbed a bus pan and cloth and began to clear the table.

"You missed Mrs. Sternau this morning," Maggie said.

"Oh, damn, that's right, today's Thursday," Troy said. It was rare that he didn't work on Thursday mornings, the day that Mrs. Sternau had been coming to the diner religiously for many years. "How's she doing?"

"She seems well," Maggie said. "But she said to tell you she was sorry she missed you. She also said to let you know the door you fixed for her is working much better now, and to ask if you had time to help her cut some branches that are growing too close to her house."

"Yeah, of course," he agreed. "I'd do just about anything to help that lady."

Customers were finishing their meals and preparing to leave while Troy and the others were cleaning tables, and refilling condiments, sugar jars, salt and pepper shakers, and setting up the coffee machines for the next morning. Troy smiled as he couldn't help but overhear the laughter and banter between Theo and Max who were working in the kitchen. Even though the money wasn't great, Troy felt the diner was a good place to work—at least for the time being. He just wished that he had a better sense of what he wanted to do when he finished college. He wanted to build a life that he hoped to share with Maggie but felt the burden of adulthood that seemed to have landed abruptly at his feet. If he had been paying attention he might have seen it coming. At least he wasn't drinking anymore, he reassured himself, and he hadn't been in a fight for over a year. As far as school was concerned, he was doing pretty well at the community college, and unless something bad happened, he still had time to make up for lost time.

The last of their work was done. "Meet you at my house?" Maggie asked.

"Sounds good to me."

They stopped to say goodbye to Theo who was collecting leftover pieces of bread to scatter in the parking lot for the birds. It was the final thing he did at the end of each workday. As if they knew when to expect him, the birds swooped in a noisy flurry from nearby trees and roofs where they waited. It was hard to tell who was happier, Theo or the birds.

"This heat's insane!" Maggie said as they stepped into the stifling hot air.

"It'll cool down," Troy said, just as rumblings of thunder rolled in from the distance.

"Let's get home ahead of the rain," she said.

It wasn't far to the house Maggie shared with two of her friends from school. They were taking classes through the summer semester and waiting tables at night at one of the fancy restaurants in the next town. Maggie's schedule was the reverse of theirs, so they only crossed paths now and then. It was a mixed bag of missing time with her friends and having the house to herself.

~

(However) by committing wholesome actions,
Which are (motivated by aspiration) in the mind,
Wherever I go I shall be presented with
Tokens of the fruit of that merit.
VII. 42

Troy slammed his door shut; the sound dulled within the dense, muggy air. His hurried footsteps kicked trails of dust from the dirt driveway. He carried the easel under his arm, and his shirt clung to his back where patches of perspiration had changed the fabric from light green to dark. A gust of wind came from the east, and the easel lifted under his grip as he broke into a run and made it to the cover of the front porch just as the sky opened into a torrential rain.

"Impressive sprint, Troy," Maggie teased. "Aren't you glad you started running with me?"

"Don't start, Mags." Troy would never agree that he was enjoying running for exercise. It was fun when he was an athlete playing team sports, but those days came to an end after high school. He never managed to get the grades in college to play college sports. Not because he couldn't have earned them, but because he was busy doing other things; many that he came to regret. But he agreed with Maggie that they needed to take care of themselves if they wanted to be in as good health as Mrs. Sternau by the time they got to be her age. So, a few evenings each week he ran at the track with Maggie, and although he wasn't admitting it, he felt some benefits like more strength and endurance.

"Here's a present from Abe," Troy said, standing the easel inside the foyer.

"Oh, I love it! I can definitely use this." She adjusted one of the legs on the easel. "I'll keep it in my car. I can't tell you how often I've been out someplace and seen something I'd like to paint. I always think I'll go back another time with an easel and paints, but of course I never get around to it."

"Where are some of the places you'd go?"

"I'd like to paint the salt marshes up the coast for instance, or there's a meadow I found in the park with a stream and gorgeous moss-covered rocks. Come to think of it, I'd really love to paint a series of Mrs. Sternau's gardens." Maggie braided her hair and wrapped an elastic around the end. "Do you think she'd mind if I spent a few afternoons there? I remember the light in her gardens that afternoon we had tea with her. It was so beautiful and peaceful there. I'd like to see if I could capture that feeling."

Troy too remembered the way the light lit the beds of daylilies. "I think she'd love it. Just ask her. She's definitely not shy about speaking her mind."

"Yeah, you're right. Okay, I will."

Maggie filled two glasses of water and handed one to Troy. "C'mon, let's go sit on the porch. My feet are in desperate need of a rest."

They sat side by side on the wicker bench with their feet on the old lobster crate that served as a coffee table.

"Abe's going to introduce me to a friend of his who knows a lot about the dharma, and who I'm hoping will be willing to teach me. His name's Jules. He's a luthier, and is the same guy Abe took my guitar to when he had some work done on the Les Paul for me."

"What's a luthier?"

"A luthier's a really specialized craftsperson who can build guitars and other stringed instruments. They can basically do anything that needs doing to repair them, make them sound better, and things like that."

"That sounds interesting. You'd probably like to learn how to do that too, wouldn't you?"

"Yeah, actually, I would." He put his arm around Maggie and drew her closer to him. "I don't want to get my hopes up yet though. Abe will let me know whether or not the guy's even willing to meet with me."

"Well, I hope it's a 'yes,'" she said.

"I do too," he said. "Do you still want to do this, Mags? I mean, study dharma with me?"

"Maybe," she said. "Let's first see how it goes with you and Jules, and whether or not I can even fit it in with the other stuff I'm doing. I have a few paintings I want to work on, and I've got to earn as much money as possible this summer to be ready for next semester." She looked at Troy, "Would you be disappointed if I didn't get into the dharma the way you're doing it?"

"Um, not thoroughly disappointed. I mean it's something that someone either feels drawn to or they don't. And, even if you're drawn to it, if now doesn't feel like the time for you, I don't expect you to live your life according to my time table."

"Well, can you at least share the things you're learning with me?"

"Sure, I can do that." Truthfully, he had been looking forward to having Maggie join him in his deeper study, but he reminded himself once again how readily things change. There are some things that there is just no point resisting. However, there was a nagging concern that was beginning to weigh on Troy's mind. Could he deepen his dharma practice and still have a regular life filled with things like his relationship with Maggie, his music, and a potential career—whatever that was going to be. It felt as if he was beginning to live a dual life. Not in a duplicitous way, but there was a sense of slipping back and forth between two different worlds. The challenge would be how to live a life where dharma practice was present in all his activities, no matter what.

"Changing the subject," he announced, "my mom's moving, and if she gets the place she's hoping for, she's invited me to move in with her. She said there's a room I could use that has its own entrance. I'll take a look at it with her on Saturday."

"No way! That's fantastic. But you know who's going to be really sad, don't you?"

"Yeah, I know—Natalie. I thought about that too. But once she sees that I don't disappear from her life, she'll be okay. I'll still do things with her. I'll take her to her piano lessons and stuff like that."

"She loves when you take her to her lessons. Actually, I think she loves doing just about anything that means she can hang out with you."

"I think you're right," he smiled, "I'm not sure how I earned her admiration, but she's definitely won my heart."

Just as men will guard their eyes
When great danger and turmoil occur,
Likewise, I shall never be swayed by the disturbances with my mind,
Even at times of great strife.
VII. 61

On Saturday morning, Troy folded the blanket he used as a cushion with extra care as he considered the things Abe had said the day before, including the importance of motivation. The easy-to-say motivation but difficult for most to fathom is the long-range goal to achieve enlightenment for the sake of all beings. This is the ultimate, altruistic goal of the Bodhisattva. A Bodhisattva is someone who is moved by love and compassion, and recognizes that their own and others' ultimate well-being depends on themselves achieving enlightenment. So, the Bodhisattva makes the commitment to achieve enlightenment for that purpose. This is the highest kind of compassion. Like anything that requires a great deal of effort and commitment, it helps to reduce the goal into smaller, more manageable steps. For Troy, this meant striving to truly comprehend what it means to develop wisdom, and to nurture the quality of mind that engages in actions rooted in compassion and wisdom.

Seated on the cushion near the window, Troy took in the view of the woods where sunlight turned a blanket of pine needles gold.

Bringing his attention to his breath, Troy followed his cycle of breathing as each breath gave birth to the next. Then as each thought gave birth to the next, he gently guided his thoughts back to the task of following his breath. It seemed as if it should be so very simple, yet the mind is powerful and easily distracted by thoughts. Distracting thoughts are strengthened by a mind that runs unobserved and unaware of its activity. However, since the mind can also be strengthened into its most powerful state by training it to focus, Troy's first step was to clear his mind of distracting thoughts by holding his attention on his breath. With each cycle of breath, he exhaled negativities such as attachment and anger, and inhaled something in the vein of blessings, which he imagined as light. If Maggie were doing the practice with him, since spirituality for her was rooted in nature, he would have suggested that she choose something from the natural environment that she felt was representative of ultimate goodness and peace. Some days this practice went more easily for Troy than others. On this particular morning, he was able to keep his mind on his breath, counting several cycles of inhalations and exhalations. He wasn't even distracted by the fact that he was succeeding until he reached the seventh. When his focus was interrupted by distracting thoughts he simply brought his attention back to his breath.

Once his mind felt settled and calm, he turned his focus to contemplate the Four Noble Truths that Abe had reviewed with him the day before. To reflect on suffering might seem like a risky and negative place to focus the mind until you understand that to see the truth of suffering serves several purposes. One is to help cultivate compassion for all living beings that are suffering. Another is to analyze the causes of specific sufferings so that you can skillfully avoid creating them. Then, by understanding the cause of your own suffering, you strengthen the wish to emerge from suffering, eventually leading to such a strong wish to be free that you develop renunciation of this suffering existence. This also allows you to realize that not only you, but all others are in the same boat of suffering existence and wish to be free from it and to experience happiness. This leads to a strong feeling of compassion not only for yourself but for others, and results in the wish for everyone to be free from suffering. As Troy went one-by-one through each of the four truths of suffering, causes of suffering, cessation of suffering, and the truth of the path, he mentally revisited Abe's explanation and thought more deeply about each.[1]

The purpose of meditation is to familiarize the mind with something positive or virtuous. Our minds are already familiar with many negative habits of thought that produce anxiety, distraction, and other negative states. A meditation practice like Troy was doing would generate the opposite by first familiarizing his mind with an accurate understanding of a positive object of meditation, and then resting his mind with a very strong focus on that understanding. The

---

1 This type of meditation is called analytical meditation. Once one has a clear and focused understanding of the object of meditation, contemplating it from many angles based on reasoning and on one's own experiences, in this case the meaning of each of the Four Noble Truths, one then moves the mind to rest single-pointedly on one's insight into or understanding of that subject, informed by its true meaning, no longer analyzing it. This is called calm abiding meditation. Through repeated meditation sessions, as one gets more and more familiar with the object, one moves into a deeper experience of the object, eventually moving to a calm abiding, single-pointed experience of the object whereby the subject (oneself as the meditator) and the object become one. In other words, one's mind completely takes on the qualities of the object, no longer seeing it as separate from oneself. Like pouring water into water. For some, this may take a very long time to be experientially realized and for others may happen quickly, depending on the amount of accumulated merit and virtue through previous study and practice, meaning from previous lifetimes. John Cerullo, Consulting Editor

repetition of this type of experience would then serve to inform his actions of mind, body, and speech with more wisdom. As a result, he could begin to bring about greater peace for himself and also, to varying degrees, for those around him.

~

I shall have to overcome
The boundless faults of myself and others,
And (in order to destroy) each of these faults (alone)
(I may have to strive until) an ocean of aeons is exhausted.
VII. 33

Troy's mother was already standing outside waiting for him when he pulled into the drive. "Good morning, honey. Let's take my car. No offense, but mine's a little cleaner than yours."

"No offense taken, Mom."

"You can have my spot. I'll meet you over there," she pointed to the corner just behind the building where her white Nissan was parked.

"You got it," he said. He waited and watched while she made her way to the car, walking a little more slowly than she had in the past. She had put on some weight in recent years, not a lot, but enough that Troy noticed. It's hard to tell which came first, the slowing down or the weight, but he hoped that she would feel something like a new enthusiasm for life once she got into her new place.

He jogged the short distance to his mother's car and climbed into the seat. "I'm not used to sitting so low," he remarked, fastening his seatbelt as they drove up the small hill back to the road. "And you're right, Mom, your car is definitely cleaner than mine," he looked to the back over his shoulder, "don't you ever just toss something into the backseat and forget about it?"

"Sure, I do, it's just that I cleaned it the other day," she laughed. "Don't be too impressed."

They followed the main road through the shopping area in town and then past the street where Maggie lived. At the four-way intersection, Troy's mother turned in the direction of his father's house and then quickly turned at the next road that wound its way around several curves flanked by stonewalls and houses on lots with willows, and massive oak and ash trees that dwarfed the homes they grew near to. It was one of the older neighborhoods that, other than the size of its trees, hadn't changed much over the past thirty years.

"Here it is," Rita said, slowing to turn onto a gravel driveway. "Isn't it perfectly charming?"

"You took the words right out of my mouth, Mom," Troy teased. "Yes, and it looks like it's really quiet here. You definitely belong in a quieter place than where you've been."

"Look," she reached in front of Troy, pointing to a slope beyond his window, "there's even a little stream. I wonder if I'll be able to hear it from the cottage. I hope so."

Next to the cottage, railroad ties marked off the parking area. Rita pulled in slowly, "See, there's room for both our cars here. And, if Maggie comes to visit, well, she'll just have to block one of us in, that's all."

They left the car and walked over the fieldstone steps that led to the front door. "The landlord said he'd leave the door unlocked for us." Before she opened the door, she stopped and pointed to the side of the house, "There's the entrance I was telling you about that you can use. See the little porch there? There's even space for a couple of chairs and maybe a very small table. And, listen." She was quiet for a moment. "Listen to those birds. Aren't they just the sweetest?" Tears filled her eyes; Troy had grown up understanding what his mother called her "happy tears" and grew to love them; especially in contrast to the sad tears he had seen during the time of his parents' divorce and when she thought he wasn't looking. Standing with her as she opened the front door and feeling her joy, he felt tears come to his eyes too.

Their voices followed them in dim echoes through the empty rooms as Rita led Troy on a tour of the cottage. It was, as she had said, small. In fact, if he were just an inch or so taller he would have needed to duck in order to clear the doorways from one room into the next.

"So, this is the living room; I like that it's so open to the kitchen. We could even have Thanksgiving here if we can talk your brothers into making the trip. There's no dining room, but look how much space there is in the kitchen. If they do come, we can add a leaf to the table. We'll be snug but everyone could fit." She rubbed her fingers along one of the windows to feel for gaps where the edges met the frame. "The windows are pretty old. We'll have to do something about the draft in the winter. But at least we'll get plenty of light."

"I saw the fireplace in the living room. Does it work?"

"I don't know, I'll have to check with the landlord."

"Natalie's piano teacher heats her house with a wood stove. It kicks out a lot of heat. Maybe you could get an insert for the fireplace; it might help."

"We'll see," she tugged on the sleeve of his shirt. "Come see the other rooms."

"Here's where you can stay." They stood together in the center of the room. "You could put your bed over there, and there's room for a dresser and a bookcase or something. What do you think?"

"It's nice, Mom." He opened the door that led out to the small porch and stepped outside. "I like it."

"I thought you might," she said, leading him out from the room again. The space from where the other rooms opened was barely long enough to call a hallway. "Here's the bathroom, and there's the room where I'll set up my sewing machine; and over here's my bedroom. None of the closets are very large, but here's one we can use for towels and linens. I love the old glass doorknobs."

"It's great, Mom. Are you sure you won't mind me living here with you? I mean, what about when I'm practicing guitar? Will that bother you?"

"Are you kidding? I love hearing you play. Unless you've become a heavy metal guy or something, I'm never bothered by your music. I love it most when you play your acoustic, but as long as you don't crank the amp super loud it's okay."

"Wait 'til you hear the Les Paul I got. You might change your mind about the acoustic being your favorite. It's got an amazing tone."

"I can't wait. Truly." She rubbed an area of his back as she had done since before he could remember. Troy imagined it was probably the area behind his heart, and now that he was old enough to make the connection, he found it interesting that this was the place her hands intuitively touched.

They left through the front door and walked around to the back of the cottage. Troy looked up to the sky, gauging the arc of the sun. "I wonder if this gets enough light for a garden. What do you think?"

"It might. What are you thinking about growing?"

"I don't know. Just a few vegetables like tomatoes and cucumbers or something."

"Well, I think it's probably too late to start a garden this season, but you can give it a try. Maybe you can find some things you can grow in pots and that are already started."

"Good idea."

"I've got to write a check for the landlord; my purse is in the car. Are you ready to go, or do you want to look around some more?"

"I want to go check out the stream," he said. "I'll be right back."

It was a shallow stream, with just enough water moving through it to see the current as it swirled around rocks and clumps of ferns and skunk cabbage. Tiny minnows darted under the sunlit water, and insects skimmed its surface pressing little circles that vanished as quickly as they appeared. Judging by the height of the banks, Troy could see where the water would rise and could carry more force. He reached into his pocket and fished out a penny before he crouched down to honor an old ritualized superstition of his and Jason's, and lowered the penny into the stream as he made a wish. In the past he would have wished for things like that a certain girl would like him, or that his father would come to his senses and realize he had made a bad mistake by marrying Maureen. But this time his wish was for his mother; that she would be happy in her new place and that the things she hoped for would be within reach. Then he remembered that, based on all he had been learning, to limit his good wishes to one person was an unwise waste of the wish, so he broadened it to include the happiness for all. When he saw his mother walking back to her car, he left the stream to join her.

"Ready?" she asked.

"Yup."

"The landlord said they'd have painters come this week and that we can begin moving things in after they're finished. We officially have the place as of the first of the month."

"Are you happy?" Troy asked.

"At this point I'm mostly overwhelmed by all that has to be done, but I'm happy thinking about how nice it will be once I'm moved in and settled."

"You'll have help, Mom. Maggie and I will help you, and I'll get in touch with Kyle."

"Thanks, Troy. I appreciate that."

The rain that had continued through Friday made for a cool morning, and as the sun climbed higher so did the temperature, but with the relief of much less humidity. They drove through town with the windows open; the music from passing cars pulsing like a universal heartbeat.

"Are you hungry? Do you want to come in for something to eat?" Rita asked as they rounded the curve just ahead of her apartment complex.

"I'd love to, Mom, but I've got to get back to Dad's. I want to catch him before he heads out and let him know I'll be moving."

"How do you think that'll go?" she asked.

"I think it'll be fine. I mean; he knows how things have been with Maureen. It'll probably be a relief. Besides, it's not like I'm moving across the country. Although, I think he'd be happier if I did. He thinks I should be packing in adventures and checking out other places."

"And what do you think? Is that something you want to do?" she asked.

"Of course I do. Ideally, I'd like to do it with Maggie. It's just that I've got to dig out from my debt, and we both want to finish school."

"How much longer 'til you're finished?" she asked, pulling into the open spot next to Troy's truck.

"I can probably wrap up my degree in two more semesters—maybe three at the most. Maggie might be done before I am."

"That's not so bad. It'll go fast, I can promise you that," she said, climbing out of the car.

"You know, Mom," he laughed, "I'm not sure if that's a good thing or a bad thing, but I'm sure you're right."

"If you fill the time with good stuff, it'll be a good thing; don't worry," she said. "I know you're a thinker, but sometimes we thinkers have to be a little more selective about the things we think about!"

"Thanks for the reminder," he said. "I'll call you later, okay?"

"Alright—I'll be here all day packing and stacking boxes."

~

Although people work in order to be happy,
It is uncertain whether or not they will find it;
But how can those whose work itself is joy
Find happiness unless they do it?
VII. 64

Both cars were in the driveway when Troy arrived at his father's house, which meant everyone was still home. He walked through the backyard and past the rose plant he had brought to Maureen just a little over a month ago. Still in the porcelain planter Mrs. Sternau had given him, it had filled out nicely with plenty of red blooms.

Natalie left her doll on the table along with her half-eaten bowl of cereal when she saw Troy come in the back door. "Hi, Troy!"

"Natalie, get back here and finish your breakfast," Maureen said. "We have to leave soon." And then, "Troy, are you hungry?"

Eyeing the bowl of fruit on the counter, "I'll have a banana, if that's okay."

"Sure," she said. "Help yourself. There are bagels, too."

"Thanks." He began peeling the banana. "Where's my Dad?"

"He's upstairs," she said. "Two more bites, Natalie. Swim class starts in twenty minutes. I don't know why they start these classes so goddamn early."

"Troy, do you want to come to swimming lessons with me?" Natalie asked.

"I've got to talk to Dad for a few minutes." He turned to Maureen and asked, "How long do the lessons last? Maybe I could pick her up, I can go early and watch some of the class."

Maureen looked at the clock on the kitchen wall, "Actually, that would be a huge help. Class is over at 11:00."

"Okay, Nat, I'll get to the beach before the end of your class and watch you swim."

"It's 'Natalie,' remember? She's not a goddamned gnat," Maureen grumbled. "But, yeah, thanks for picking her up. I have a hair appointment."

"No problem. And have a good class, Natalie," Troy tugged on her ponytail. "I'll see you in a little while."

"I'll do a flip off the float for you," she said.

"Can't wait," Troy said as he walked from the room to find his father. "I want to swim too, so we'll hang out at the beach after your class."

"Make sure you put sunscreen on her, Troy. I'll kill you if she comes home with a burn."

"Got it," Troy said, already halfway down the hall.

"And tell your father to give you money so you can buy Natalie lunch," she yelled after him.

"Will do," he called from the staircase that wound in a spiral around the chandelier Troy considered to be one of the hallmarks of Maureen's pretentious taste in decorating.

"Dad?"

"Yeah, I'm in here." Troy followed his father's voice to his bedroom.

"Where were you this morning?" Brian asked.

"I was with Mom."

"Since when is she a morning person?"

"I don't know, I never knew she wasn't," Troy answered. "Anyway, she's moving. She wanted to show me her new place."

"Where's she moving to?"

"To a place on one of the roads off Topstone; it's an old neighborhood. It's really quiet and I think she'll be happy there. In fact, I know she can't wait to get out of that apartment," Troy said.

"Good." His father tucked his shirt into his shorts and tightened his belt. "I hope it works out for her."

"Well, she got a promotion at work, so she can afford the higher rent. The place is a small cottage; it has a little yard and some privacy. She's excited to get her sewing machine set up again," Troy said, doling out the information in increments to pave the way for the news that he, too, would be moving.

Brian pulled a pair of socks from his drawer. "Don't let Maureen hear me say this, but I'm glad your mom's getting out of that apartment." He sat on the king-sized bed, slowly unrolling the socks from the ball they'd been stored in, "It's always bothered me that, well, you know," his voice trailed off, "oh, forget it. I just wish it could've been different, that's all."

"I know," Troy answered, even though he hadn't really known, and at this point, he wasn't sure he wanted to know. "The cottage has three bedrooms. One of them has its own entrance, and she's invited me to stay there."

"And?" He sat upright, with one sock on and the other sock dangling, as if forgotten. "What was your answer?"

"Well, that's why I went to look at it this morning." Troy sat down on the bed next to his father. "It's a nice spot, and it's really close by." He hesitated before saying more. "Maureen and I have been getting along better, and I know she's trying really hard from her end. We've even had a couple of heart-to-heart conversations. I just think it'll be easier all around if I'm not living here, Dad. Besides, it's not as if I'm going around the world or something."

"Yeah, I know," he put the other sock on and grunted as he reached for the pair of sneakers on the floor. "So, when's the move date?"

"First of the month." Troy looked at the framed photograph of Natalie on his father's dresser, "Natalie's not gonna be happy about this, but I'll stay close and do stuff with her."

"She'll be okay," Brian said, tying his shoelaces. "I mean, it's life, right? The earlier you learn to roll with things the better off you'll be when the shit really hits the fan." He planted a firm pat with a thump on Troy's back, a different touch from his mother's, but the same spot she had gently rubbed earlier, "Because, inevitably the shit always hits the fan, right?"

"It sure as hell does," Troy laughed.

Brian stood from the bed and turned toward the dresser where he kept his wallet and keys, "I told Fred I'd meet him at the driving range." He swung an imaginary golf club, slicing it through the air, and laughed, "he thinks I can help him with his swing." He slid his wallet into his back pocket, and dropped his keys into his hip pocket.

"Okay, have a good time," Troy said. "I'll see you later."

"Do you want to join us?" Brian asked.

"Thanks, but not today. I told Natalie I'd pick her up from her swimming lesson. Maybe another time?"

"Sure. See you later."

"Yup. See ya."

Troy went to his room, rifled through his drawers to find a bathing suit, changed his clothes and then grabbed a beach towel from the hall closet. He headed downstairs and was on his way out the front door when he remembered the sunscreen. He was pretty sure Maureen wouldn't have let Natalie go to the beach without it, but wasn't about to take any chances on inciting Maureen's rage, so went back upstairs and rummaged through the bathroom closet where he found about five different bottles to choose from. He took the one with the highest number on its label and ran down the stairs and out the door.

~

Thus in order to complete this task,
I shall venture into it
Just as an elephant tormented by the mid-day sun
Plunges into a (cool, refreshing) lake.
VII. 66

Troy rolled his t-shirt, keys, wallet and the bottle of sunscreen into his towel and left it with his sandals on a patch of sand near the stone jetty. He walked to the water's edge where he spotted Natalie standing in a circle with the others in her class, waist deep in the water as they watched their teacher demonstrate the motions of the forward crawl. The beach was filling with families toting coolers, beach chairs, and colorfully striped beach umbrellas to spend the day. Children raced to the water; some carrying buckets and shovels to begin their day's industry of digging moats, building castles and waterways, a project that would require a great deal of engineering to withstand the changing tide.

Troy dove into the water and didn't surface until after he'd made it most of the way to the float and then swam with long strokes all the way to the buoys where he turned onto his back and floated. For the moment there was no place he needed to go or anything he needed to do. It felt good to float, weightless, in the salt water while the shallow waves rocked him in a lazy rhythm that was as constant as his own breath. Everything seemed to speak of peace, even the occasional humming of planes that appeared only as tiny slivers sliding through the rich blue sky. It was hypnotic, he thought, but then, just that thought itself interrupted the trance and he began thinking about jellyfish that could be lurking nearby and imagined their stinging tentacles sloshing around his ankles or slipping under his arms. As he swam back toward shore, eyes peeled for jellyfish, he was amused by the awareness that this was the experience of daily life: the things that disturb one's peace arise in the untrained mind with an immediacy that feels as if it's outer-driven, yet it's the unexamined reactivity of the mind that gets the ball rolling.

Natalie and the others in her class swam with their teacher in loose formation to the float. Troy smiled, amused as he watched from the beach; he thought the children looked like newly hatched turtles with only their shiny wet heads poking above the water's surface as they paddled away. Once he saw that Natalie was safely on the float, he curved his fingers to his lips and whistled, a piercing whistle that she instantly recognized as his. She waved and yelled, "Troy, watch!" and with a quick run to the edge, she flipped off the side of the float into the water, disappearing with barely a trace. Just as quickly, she bobbed to the surface, and then dogpaddled around to the ladder and climbed to join the other kids. Troy raised his arms high with a two thumbs-up approval.

Soon the class was over and the children swam back to shore where they waited for their parents. Natalie ran to Troy and gave him a wet, salty hug, dripping water from her ponytail and the straps that fastened her bathing suit behind her neck.

"Are you hungry?" Troy asked, offering her his towel.

"No," she said.

"Yeah, well, you will be soon," he ruffled the top of her head making bumps in her wet hair. "Besides, I'm hungry. Let's go to the concession stand before it gets crowded."

"Okay, but I've got to get my stuff." She ran to the bench under the tree where all the kids had left their things during class, grabbed the pink and yellow polka-dot canvas bag Maureen had packed for her, and then, kicking sand in her wake, ran back to where Troy stood waiting. As they walked together, Natalie reached for Troy's hand, hopping and skipping to match his stride.

"Great flip, by the way, Nat."

"Thanks. They're fun to do. Do you want me to teach you how?"

"Um, maybe. There's a lot more of me that would need to roll up into the right shape for a flip, I'm not sure I could pull it off."

Natalie stopped walking to examine her brother's height. "I see what you mean. It might be tricky."

They carried their lunch on trays to the pavilion where seagulls were congregating by garbage bins and under picnic tables to feast on scraps of food. Troy and Natalie chose a table further away, but one that was closest to a view of the water.

They sat side-by-side, dipping their fries into a white paper cup filled with ketchup, watching wisps of clouds unfurl in slow motion within the azure sky.

"You've never met my mom, have you, Natalie?"

"Nope. Is she nice?"

"Super nice," he said. "Except sometimes when we were kids and my brothers and I were causing trouble."

"Why'd you do that?" she asked, resting her head against the hand that wasn't busy dipping and eating fries, one after another."

"We didn't do it on purpose. Usually, we were just playing around, but sometimes we'd get out of hand." Troy laughed, "Actually, it was more like lots of times."

"I wish your brothers lived with us."

"Yeah, well, I miss having them around, too, but they're busy working and stuff. That's what happens, right? I mean, everyone grows up and has to work at something, and sometimes people work in places different from where the rest of their family lives."

"Why doesn't my mom like your mom?"

"Hmmm. That's probably hard for us to know for sure." Everything was so matter-of-fact for Natalie. Troy couldn't give her the matter-of-fact explanation that Maureen had met their father while he was still married to Rita, and that that's just an impossible scenario for anyone to come through unscathed. He remembered the ugliness of it all very well, but didn't want Natalie to have to be touched by it, certainly not on his watch.

"Well," he said, "my mother is moving to a new house. It's actually close to your house," he began.

Natalie interrupted him, "It's your house, too."

"Well, not really. But I get to stay there if I need to, which is really nice." He spooned some coleslaw onto Natalie's plate. "Since my mother lives alone, and now that she is moving to a bigger house, she's asked me if I would like to live there with her."

"No!" Natalie yelled, her eyes filling with tears. "If you do that, I won't see you anymore!"

"Of course, you'll see me," Troy reassured her. "I'll only be living a few streets away from you! I'll still come visit you at your house. And, I'll take you to piano lessons, swimming lessons, or wherever," he smiled, "I love you Nat; we'll always see each other."

Natalie stopped eating and frowned, mulling everything over that Troy had just told her.

"Do you promise?" she asked, wiping a tear from the corner of her eye with the back of her hand.

"I promise," he said, reaching his hand toward hers and extending his pinky finger, "pinky-swear."

She did the same, and their hooked pinkies sealed the deal. She dipped another fry in the ketchup and took a bite, "Don't forget," she added for good measure.

"I won't."

~

Maureen was home when Troy returned with Natalie. She was in good spirits, having just come back from getting her hair done, a manicure, pedicure—the whole treatment. Her skin was glowing, she told Natalie, because she had just had the most marvelous and relaxing facial, and she promised Natalie that for her next birthday she would take her to have one too. Troy decided this was a perfect time to tell Maureen about his plans. She was rarely so relaxed and pleasant. Maybe her efforts to change really had begun to have some effect. When he told her that he'd be moving to share the new place with his mother at the beginning of August, she said she thought that would be a nice change for everyone.

Things were falling into place. Now it was a matter of waiting to hear whether or not Jules would agree to teach him.

~

Thus in order to increase my enthusiasm
I should strive to abandon its opposing forces,
To (amass the supports of) aspiration, self-confidence, joy and rest,
To Practice in earnest and to become strong in self control.
VII. 32

Troy and his mother spent the week following the move unpacking and getting settled into the cottage. Troy filled his room with his bed, a dresser, a bookshelf, an amp, and hung his three guitars from mounts he installed on the wall. By the time he was finished, it was a tight fit with very little walking space. Maggie had spent most of her free time at the cottage with Troy and his mother, helping to get all the odds and ends sorted out. The day Troy moved the furniture from his father's house, Maureen and Natalie gave him a pot of red geraniums to keep on the porch outside his bedroom. Maureen said they'd be easy for him to keep alive and would keep flowering into the fall. This or any other gesture of kindness would never have occurred just two months earlier, and Maureen's tentativeness as she helped Natalie hold the plant steady while she gave it to Troy carried a hint of warmth that caught them both slightly off guard. Although still fragile, the softening in their relationship was opening.

By the end of the following weekend, Rita had finished organizing the drawers and cupboards in the kitchen. She filled a ceramic vase with coneflowers and daisies she had taken from the garden for the table, and on Monday morning announced that along with the smell of eggs, toast, and coffee, the cottage was beginning to feel like home.

Even though she had been imagining an ideal sewing room for years, she saved tackling that room for last. She told Troy that she was going to think it through a little more, and that it was a matter of adapting her vision to the space this particular room offered. Several boxes were stacked against the wall where she planned to install shelves for storing fabric and other supplies, and her sewing machine, still in its case, was on top of its table. She couldn't wait to begin working on her first project; it was either going to be a quilt, or something she could wear; she hadn't yet made up her mind. Whatever it would be, she had the urge to try something elaborate. For now, it would all have to wait until the next weekend as it was the beginning of another week at work where she was still adjusting to the responsibilities that came along with her new position at the nursing home.

Troy arrived late to work and had barely finished doing the set-up when the breakfast customers began to arrive, noisily dragging chairs against the floor as they took their seats. Later in the morning, when things slowed down, he checked his phone and saw that he had missed a call from Abe. He immediately ducked into the alcove just outside the kitchen to return his call.

"Hey, Abe, it's Troy. I just saw you called."

"Good news! I heard from Jules yesterday. Sorry it took a while. It turns out he was doing a retreat, but he's back now and said to tell you to give him a call and the two of you can work out how you'll get together."

"Fantastic!" Troy said. "What's his number?" Troy reached around the corner to grab a pen and an order pad from the counter, and scribbled down the number as Abe gave it to him.

"He said you can reach him either later today or tomorrow morning after nine-thirty; he'll be working in his studio all day."

"Great. I'll try him as soon as I can." Troy tore the page with Jules' number on it from the pad and folded it into his back pocket. "Thanks Abe, I'll let you know how it goes after I reach him."

"Sounds good. You'll find he's someone you can learn a lot from."

"I'm sure you're right," Troy said. "I'll be in touch; thanks again."

"Happy to help. Bye."

Troy took the piece of paper with Jules' number from his pocket again, remembering that when he first met Abe he had insisted Troy memorize his phone number and wouldn't let him simply store it in his phone. That was the beginning of Abe teaching him about the importance of training his mind, to strengthen its ability to focus and also about the importance of being vigilant to the quality of his thoughts. Thoughts are actions of the mind, and Abe had explained that negative actions of mind, body, and speech all create karmic imprints that eventually ripen into active negative habits that, unless eliminated, grow stronger. He told Troy to think of karma like a game of pool, his life as the cue ball, and his thoughts as the cue. In a game of pool, you evaluate the table, how and where you stand, and then carefully align the cue before taking your shot. Similarly, in life you can develop a practice of mindfulness, including awareness of things like motivation and intention, so that you can aim skillfully with any action you take, including thoughts and speech. The change in his relationship with Maureen was evidence of the power that came from mindfully directing his actions in a skillful way.

"What's up?" Maggie asked.

"I just talked to Abe. He gave me the number for Jules, that guy I was telling you about. He said he'd meet with me—I just need to call him to figure out when."

"That's great," Maggie said. "You must be so excited!"

"I'm actually a little nervous, Mags, but yeah, I'm definitely excited. There's so much I want to get my head around and understand better. I know I've barely begun to scratch the surface of what this adventure really holds."

The dharma comes to life little by little when it includes study, reflection, and the actual practice of putting what has been learned into action in one's daily life. Like three strands of a braid, they overlap and strengthen each other, and as one's experience deepens, questions arise that require yet more study, reflection and, meditation. After his recent visit with Abe, Troy stopped agonizing over where to begin because he realized that in essence he had already begun, and at this point it was a matter of working with the strands he already had in hand, recognizing they're all part of one braid. However, he didn't want this to be something that he lived separately from his daily life. But with all there was to learn, and the amount of time and energy he felt was necessary to devote to study and practice, how could he do it all? This was one of the things he hoped Jules would shed some light on—a way to incorporate the dharma into his entire life, whether he was actually studying and practicing dharma or participating in the rest of his normal life endeavors.

"When are you going to call him?" Maggie asked. "Can you call him now?"

Troy looked at the number again, smiled, and said, "After I get home, and as soon as I've memorized his phone number."

"Ah," Maggie laughed, "Abe taught you well!"

~

Whoever seizes self-confidence in order to conquer
the enemy of self-importance,
They are the self-confident ones, the victorious
heroes,
And in addition, whoever definitely conquers the
spread of this enemy, self-importance,
Completely (wins) the fruit of a Conqueror, fulfilling
the wishes of the world.
VII. 59

The next morning, Troy made a point to get out of bed earlier than he had the day before and prepared for his meditation practice. Instead of the folded blanket he had been using, he used the cushion Maggie had given him. She told him that her favorite gifts were those given for no particular occasion and that the other day, when she had seen the cushion in a small boutique in town, she wanted him to have it right away.

Troy didn't want to rush through his practice, especially not today. The basic routine was the same as usual, but with additional effort to calm his mind by revisiting his commitment to study and practice. Later, when he would be calling Jules, he wanted this energy to be the most present in his mind, overriding any self-doubting nervousness that could stir his mind and challenge his confidence. Self-doubt is basically an offshoot of pride, one of the many negative mental states identified by the Buddha. With that understanding, Troy could easily see that the result of self-doubt and other self-effacing habits are ultimately negative too. There's a difference between being humble and self-doubting, just as there is a difference between being confident and prideful. Being humble and confident will strengthen you, while self-doubt and pride weaken you. To support his confidence, he reviewed the progress he had made over the past several months. The previously dominant presence of anger was gradually being replaced by gentleness and peace. Even when confronted with some difficult customers at work, he skillfully carried generosity and compassion into some challenging encounters. Reflecting on these changes reinforced his confidence in his own capacity and strengthened his confidence in the dharma as well. It was through the dharma that he developed his mind to shift his perception of how any experience manifests, and, with only a preliminary understanding of karma and impermanence, he recognized his participation in creating all of his experiences. Reflecting on this was the analytical portion of his meditation practice. From here he settled into the calm abiding portion. The quality of mind produced by his analytical process became the object of his focus, where he single-pointedly held his attention. The breathing meditations he had been practicing since taking his first steps onto this path were training him to cultivate the ability to sustain a focus that was relaxed yet firm. It was in this state that Troy stayed for quite some time.

When he finished his meditation, he quietly offered a dedication directing whatever positive energy, or merit, he had created as a result of his practice to help propel him toward his goal, a goal that included the intention to benefit all sentient beings. One of the most important aspects of meditation practice, and actually in all activities, is setting one's motivation before starting, which should always be for the benefit of all others, and, at the end, dedicating the practice to benefit all others. They are the essential bookends of any meditation practice. Without them, what comes in between has not been planted properly in fertile soil—the intention being the seeds, the meditation being the planting in fertile soil, and the dedication being the watering, so the best possible results can be gained for all.

~

Troy made his coffee, and then left to get Maggie on their way to work.

Maggie's hair was wet when she came out of the house carrying her sneakers in her hands. She walked barefoot across the lawn and the gravel driveway to Troy's truck.

"Good morning, love of my life!" Maggie dropped her sneakers on the floor of the truck and wrapped her arms around Troy.

"Wow, thanks, love of mine!"

"I woke up in the middle of the night last night and couldn't get back to sleep," Maggie said. "Then I remembered hearing one of the customers mention that the Perseids were beginning soon, so I got out of bed, grabbed one of those little beach chairs from the porch, and walked outside hoping I might catch a sneak preview of them. Oh my god, Troy, it was so peaceful sitting out there, and the sky was so clear and full of stars I just hung out taking it all in like the sky and I were inseparable. I suppose we all are inseparable from the sky, aren't we?" she paused, "Ha! That's kind of a cool thought! Anyway, I heard a screech owl carrying on for a while and then, just as I'd practically given up on seeing any meteors, not just one, but two gorgeous ones shot across the sky. They looked so close it seemed like they could've just fallen into my lap!"

"Did you make a wish?" Troy asked.

"Damn, I forgot."

"Well, quick—close your eyes and watch them again in your mind and make a wish!"

Maggie closed her eyes, making her wish while Troy wished he could give her whatever it was she longed for.

~

By ten thirty, things were quiet, and Troy took the opportunity to call Jules. He went outside to the edge of the parking lot to the large rock in the shade where he often spent his breaks. He waited through several rings before Jules answered.

"Hello?"

"Hello, this is Troy Reilly, a friend of Abe's..."

"Oh, yes, Abe told me you'd be calling. What can I do for you?"

"Well, over the past several months, I've been studying, and trying to develop a dharma practice. When I told Abe I was hoping he could help me deepen my study and practice, he suggested I reach out to you."

"Why don't you come by my studio later and we can talk. Are you free, say around four o'clock either today or tomorrow?"

"Um, sure, either works. How 'bout today? Except I'm not usually finished with work until about three-thirty so it might be a little after four by the time I get to you."

"That's fine," Jules said, and then gave him the address and directions to his studio. "I'm looking forward to meeting you."

"I'm looking forward to meeting you too. See you soon."

"Oh, and hey, can you bring that Les Paul with you?"

"Sure," Troy said. "I'll stop by my house and grab it on my way."

"Sounds good."

Troy stayed on the rock a little while longer anticipating what it might be like to meet Jules. It was one thing to have just happened to meet Grace, Abe and, Mrs. Sternau who each taught him many things, but this was different. He was asking to meet Jules with the specific purpose of receiving instruction. He hoped he would measure up to whatever requirements Jules might have.

When he got back inside, Maggie and Theo were in the kitchen prepping for lunch.

"Hey, where'd you disappear to?" Theo asked.

"Sorry, Theo. I just had to make a quick call."

"No problem..." Theo put the knife on the cutting board where he had been slicing tomatoes and piling them in perfect little stacks where the tomatoes practically looked whole. "I need you to give me a hand. I want to set up a few more tables outside today. It brings more business when people drive by and see other folks eating outside. You know, the power of suggestion or something like that."

"Sure, let's do it," Troy said. "We only have a couple more months before it'll be too cold. Ya gotta make hay while the sun shines, right?"

"Making hay, making money, whatever—just so long as the sun keeps shining."

In Theo's world, no matter what was going on, it seemed the sun was always shining. His plan worked like a charm. Customers filled the tables outside and most of the tables inside as well. Troy enjoyed the extra chaos; especially the fun of joking around with the regular customers he had gotten to know. Theo turned the music up a little louder when he found a station playing his favorite old jazz tunes. The hours passed and before long the tables were mostly empty except for a few customers sipping coffee and dipping spoons into glass bowls to scrape the last traces of ice cream.

~

"I've gotta run, Mags," Troy said. "I'm heading out to meet Jules now, so I'll call you when I'm on my way back."

"I hope it goes well, although I have no doubt that it will," Maggie said.

"Thanks, Mags." As he opened the door to leave he turned to look at her and said, "I know things have been really hectic lately. I'm sorry. Now that my mom and I are moved in, things should settle down. I hope you know how much your help has meant to me; I don't want you to ever have any reason to feel I take you for granted." Before he left he asked, "How about dinner tonight?"

"It's a date," she said.

~

Self-confidence should be applied to (wholesome) actions,
The (overcoming) of disturbing conceptions and my ability (to do this).
Thinking, "I alone shall do it,"
Is the self-confidence of action.
VII. 49

Back at the cottage, Troy slid the guitar case from under his bed and carefully settled the Les Paul inside before closing the latches. He checked the clock; did he have time for a shower? He didn't want to meet Jules drenched in the scent of bacon grease and home fries and decided there was no question; time or no time he wasn't showing up without cleaning up. He was in and out of the shower in a matter of minutes, put on clean jeans, tucked in a button-down shirt, and threaded a belt through the belt loops. He didn't have time to look through the unpacked boxes stacked in the corner of his closet for a better pair of shoes, so his sandals had to do. He grabbed the guitar case and the orange book Mrs. Sternau had given him and ran out the door. As he glanced over the directions to get to Jules' studio, he thought again about his motivation. He wished it were something specific and clear that he could easily put into words. He had learned enough to know that what remained to be known was immense. His curiosity to know more was insatiable. Was he really ready for what he wanted to ask for from Jules? *Yeah I'm ready*, he told himself, arguing against the doubts that were undermining his enthusiasm. *If I want to play the guitar, I don't have to know everything about what the instrument can do before I approach a teacher. I just need to know that I want to play.*

There was plenty of time to vacillate between feelings of confidence and doubt several times over while he drove. *When in doubt, doubt the doubter,* he told himself. Check in to see who is doing the doubting, and question if the doubt serves any legitimate purpose. Using logic to unravel the doubt and the actual basis of just exactly who the doubter is moved him back toward confidence. That logic included something he'd been hearing about from his previous teachers, that nothing exists independently—free of causes and conditions—not even doubt or the person doing the doubting. By examining the source of those causes and conditions, and understanding one's own role in creating them, freedom begins to show its smiling face like a magician who senses you have glimpsed the source of his or her magic.

Troy turned onto a dirt road that led to a stone driveway with a carved wooden sign hung from a thick cedar post that said, "Julian Amaquieu, Luthier." Entering the driveway, he saw a small, one-story house and a contemporary style barn. Julian had told him earlier that the studio was in the barn and that he should let himself in when he arrived.

~

I should never indulge in despondency by entertaining
such thoughts as,
"How shall I ever awaken?"
For the Tathagatas who speak what is true
Have uttered this truth:
"If they develop the strength of their exertion
Even those who are flies, mosquitoes, bees and insects
Will win the unsurpassable Awakening,
Which is so hard to find."
VII. 17, 18

Troy breathed in the sweet scent of wood, sawdust, oils, and varnish as he slid the heavy barn door in its tracks. Spruce, burnt maple, and wood tar were an exotic tea for the air. He sensed he had entered the space of a master. Inside the barn was an impeccably clean workshop of neatly arranged chisels and calipers, multiple workbenches, a drum sander, band saw, bending iron, and drawings that looked like they could've been pages from one of DaVinci's notebooks. Violin and cello molds hung on the walls; and a few works in progress in various stages of repair or design, including a cello, opened like an anesthetized patient on one of the larger workbenches.

And there was Jules. Troy thought he looked to be about the same age as Abe, perhaps a little older and a little taller. Jules placed the small, steel blade he had been using in its tray and wiped his hands on a cloth that hung by the workbench where curls of freshly peeled wood had collected into a soft pile like a cloud of spun honey and gold.

"Welcome," Jules reached out his hand to shake Troy's. "You must be Troy; I recognize that old guitar case."

Troy tucked the book under his arm and extended his free hand to meet Jules'.

"Yes, nice to meet you, Mr...."

"Please, call me Jules."

"Okay, Jules, nice to meet you."

"Likewise," Jules said. "You can put your guitar on that bench over there," he said gesturing to the table under a row of tall windows. "Your buddy, Abe, has said good things about you."

"Well, that's nice to hear," Troy said. "I feel lucky to know him. He told me that you two go way back; that you both studied with the same teacher years ago."

"Yeah, you're right. It's weird how that seems both like yesterday and lifetimes ago at once. He and I were hanging out in Washington Square Park in the city when we first heard there was a Rinpoche teaching in New Jersey. We both began attending his teachings, and so yeah, we share a very special bond through our teacher." Jules picked up a stool and handed it to Troy, "Here— sorry I don't have something more comfortable. Let's sit over there," he said nodding toward the row of windows where Troy had left his guitar. He took another stool for himself. "What's that book you've got there?"

"Oh, a woman I've recently gotten to know gave this to me." Troy passed the thin book to Jules. "She said it was a favorite of her husband's who passed away many years ago. Her husband was a university professor, and she told me that they began studying the dharma together sometime in the 1950s. You can tell which passages were his favorites by the pages with turned down corners." He watched as Jules slowly turned each page, stopping to read some passages more closely than others.

Jules laughed and then read aloud, "Feelings are traceless like drawings on water; there is no holding on to erroneous appearances..." [2]

"What do you think that's about, Troy?" Jules asked, gently closing the book.

"Um, I think it's saying that feelings have no real substance and that's why you shouldn't get all hung up on them. They come and go, but you have to be careful because sometimes it's easy to convince yourself that they come from something outside of you and that you're helpless in the face of them; like you don't recognize your own participation in getting them going." Troy felt the heat of self-consciousness flush his face. "Feelings come about through certain types of habits,

2 *One Hundred Spiritual Instructions to the People from Pha Dampa Sangs rgyas, a Buddhist teacher who came from India to Tibet in the last part of the eleventh century. Edited and translated by Lozang Jamspal, PhD and David Kittay, PhD Ladak Ratnashridipika 2011*

right? Like habits of thought and habitual ways we see and respond to things. They're like filters that mess with how we interpret everything we experience."

"There's a lot to understand about the mind," Jules said. "Buddhism takes a very detailed investigation into the mind; we'll talk more about that in time, but you've got the right idea. You might've already heard the suggestion to think of the mind's nature as being like the sky, and things like anger, hatred, desire, and other feelings as being clouds that come and go. Or, shifting the metaphor to water, traceless like drawings on water."

Jules opened the book and looked through the pages again. "Ah! Here's a really important one," he said. "The time and opportunity given to a human body is like fine gold; don't waste it uselessly..."[3]

"This," Jules said, "is why you and I are sitting here together right now. Did you notice we didn't take time to chitchat about the weather, or how the Mets played this season? Once you really get a taste of the dharma and its ultimate and very rare value, there's an understanding that arises with a lot of strength, and

---

3 *One Hundred Spiritual Instructions to the Dingri People from Pha Dampa Sangs rgyas, a Buddhist teacher who came from India to Tibet in the last part of the eleventh century. Edited and translated by Lozang Jamspal, PhD and David Kittay, PhD Ladak Ratnashridipika 2011*

that is the acute awareness that life is precious. Life is short, we never know when it will end, and so we don't want to waste a second of it. Why is this life so precious? Well, first of all, because you were born human. That's not always a given.

"The Buddha, like other masters, often taught using parables. He said to imagine an old, blind turtle that lives at the bottom of the seven oceans and suppose this turtle comes to the surface only once every hundred years. It just so happens that there is a golden yoke—only one, mind you—that is floating around on the sea. Now, when that old, blind turtle comes up to the surface just once in a hundred years to take his breath in the midst of that incredibly vast, vast ocean, it's as likely for him to happen to put his head through the neck hole of that golden yoke as it is for anyone to be born into a human life. If you think about all the many, many insects, birds, fish, mammals, reptiles and so on there are—just on this planet alone—compared to the number of humans, you can see that their numbers are far greater than those who are human. So, even though we all admire the beauty of animals in nature, we're pretty damn lucky to have come into a human life rather than one of an animal or insect. We're not a small insect, for instance, and don't have to worry about being squashed by someone walking over us with their giant feet, or an animal that is hunted, or raised in captivity to be slaughtered for food. We have intelligence that allows us to learn and to create wonderful things. However, even if we are born human, not all humans are fortunate to be living in a place or time where there is peace, plenty of food and water, clean air, comfortable beds to sleep in, and warm, dry houses to live in. Having all those very fortunate conditions means we have tremendous freedom. A large percentage of people in the world today don't share our fortunate conditions, and they would consider ours to be a life of leisure. It gets even better if we have the opportunity to meet the dharma, to recognize its value, and to meet others who can teach and guide us as we learn and practice the dharma. From the Buddhist point of view, we didn't land here by some freak accident, Troy. Being born human means in previous lives you created the causes, or virtuous karma, for a human life through positive actions. But we can't rest on our laurels, because the way karma carries from one lifetime to another doesn't mean there aren't also traces of negative karma from countless previous lives still remaining. Once a karmic seed ripens, it's done, kaput, and that means our entire collection of karma that has not yet ripened still has the potential to take root. When we make good use of this life by cultivating mindfulness for instance and achieving a deep understanding of how karma works, we then have the capacity to create the causes for another human rebirth, or perhaps a life that offers even more freedom than that when this life comes to its end."

"Well, that's pretty disheartening, Jules. If there's no way to know what kind of karma I've been dragging along with me from one life into another, it seems like a crap shoot. I mean, you're talking about countless lives over lord knows how many eons. Who knows what my ratio of good and bad karma is that's just waiting to pop? The odds don't sound at all good."

The frown lines on Jules' face deepened, "I'm sure you've learned something about impermanence, Troy. What role do you think impermanence plays with regard to things like your previous karma, your next life being a crap shoot, and the feelings you describe as disheartening?"

"Um, I guess I need to think about that," Troy said, gazing at the floor, noting the planks of wood swept clean except where Jules had been working. "So, I know that everything is always undergoing change. Literally everything."

"Right. It's the nature of all things to change. Go on," Jules said.

"Um, yeah, it's the nature of things to change, and the way one thing feeds into another I'm wondering if impermanence is a cause or a condition, or maybe it's both?"

Jules sat quietly for a moment before he answered, his long legs crossed, one draped over the other tugging the hem of his jeans above the laced work boots and grey argyle socks. "Because impermanence is a quality of all things that arise, or we could say of 'all produced things,' then because of impermanence these things can provide the potential to be a cause, a condition, or both. So, in that regard I think it's safe to say it's both. But with this understanding of the nature of impermanence coupled with the role of wisdom and intention, then what does that do to your idea of rebirth being a crap shoot?"

Troy understood that questioning was part of learning, but he was already wishing for a reprieve. He mumbled the question softly to himself, "Is rebirth a crap shoot?" The ceiling fan spun slowly overhead marking time as he let the question settle in his mind. Jules conveyed no sense of hurry as the two sat quietly. The Four Noble Truths Troy had been reviewing since his meeting with Abe came to mind, "No, I guess it's not a crap shoot. According to The Four Noble Truths, there are causes for suffering and therefore causes to end suffering."

"Yeah, well, according to The Four Noble Truths that's true," Jules said. "And, what about according to you? What about your own experience?"

"Well, that's a little easier to answer," Troy said. "I've definitely caused a lot of problems and suffering in my own life through things I've done, and in the past several months I've made a conscious effort to do things differently, and that's making things go more smoothly."

"Okay, then," Jules said with a bit of amusement, "where does your crap shoot stand, and is it really so disheartening?"

"I still don't know about my previous karma, so yeah, I'd say it is still disheartening."

"Look at the mess on the floor over there," Jules pointed to where he had been working when Troy first came in. "I've been working by that bench for years, and if I didn't sweep the floor every day when I finished work I'd have one hell of a mess by now. I suppose if I were lazy I could just work around the mess, but if I want to turn out well-made instruments I need to keep the workspace clean so the wood and glue for instance have the purest conditions to be joined together. Life isn't all so different. We could be lazy and just let all our crap keep collecting, and if we did, then our conditions would definitely reflect that in many ways. But we have the opportunity now to do some cleaning up so we can prepare the best conditions to build from going forward. And we can do that through virtuous activities of body, speech, and mind that actually gather into something like a very positive energetic force we call 'merit.'"

Troy recalled a somewhat similar discussion he and Abe had about purifying karma. It's what he and Abe had set out to do the day they'd offered all that money to charity. "Abe taught me about the four powers of purification. I'd forgotten about that until just now. He said that if it's done with the right motivation, understanding, and commitment, you can actually purify negative karma. Sometimes I think that I'm trying to learn so much that half of what I learn gets dumped as I take in new stuff. Damn—talk about disheartening. But, that's why I'm here. I want to learn well, and I want to learn correctly. So, I may be a slow learner, but I'm a determined student."

"You're learning, Troy. Don't ever beat yourself up about whether or not you're meeting some expectation only you have constructed for yourself. You're putting forth effort and for that you can be pleased. This study and practice that you're doing isn't about finding religion or passing exams for grades, Troy—not at all. It's about making life work in the best possible way, better than you might even be able to imagine now. We're unbelievably fortunate to have met a course, or a path, that's been well tested by some amazing people who've blazed the trail ahead of us. Because it's been so carefully preserved in its purest form, we get to share in the benefit of what they discovered. As we deepen our practice and develop the right view of something presented in the dharma called 'dependent arising' or the interdependence of all things, you can't help but jump into life with a blissful attitude. You might say, 'here's where the fun begins' and understand why, in this practice, they call it joyous effort."

"Yes, joyous effort," Troy smiled. "That's exactly what Abe and I were talking about the other day!"

"It's like practicing the guitar, right?" Jules suggested. "You're drawn to pick it up when you see it, you think about music and riffs even when you're not with it. You're listening to those musicians you consider to be masters, who inspire you to practice and whose art inspires new ideas. Of course there's frustrations in the practice, the times when your fingers just don't cooperate with what you're trying to do. Those are the times when you might put the instrument down and do something else for a while. Studying and practicing dharma's not all that different. Sometimes you just have to take a rest. What you've accumulated doesn't vanish if you take a rest, but you have to know you'll come back to it, and, when you do, you'll come back to it with new energy and focus."

Jules looked at Troy's guitar case on the workbench. "Now, let's open up that case and see how your guitar's doing."

Jules opened the brown case and lifted the guitar from the pink velvet lining. "I think Abe told me this guitar stayed closed in its case for some forty years after the kid it belonged to was killed in Viet Nam. The parents never parted with it until they both died and then it came with everything Abe got from their house," Jules said, raising the guitar eye level, holding it to check the straightness of its neck. "Tragic, really," he placed the guitar on the bench; resting it on a block covered in carpeting to support the neck, "War is the world's most blatant evidence of human ignorance and its resulting suffering."

He rubbed his fingers along the fret board. "The silver lining, I suppose, is that the guitar is in pretty good shape since it's had so little wear and tear. When Abe asked me to give it a going over before he gave it to you, there were a few fine scratches I took care of, but nothing drastic. Preserving the patina is very important for a vintage guitar like this one. But I think we could replace some of the frets and make some adjustments to the neck if you'd like."

"Sure, I'd like that," Troy said. "Actually, I'd like to see how it's done; and if it's not too much trouble, maybe even learn to do some of the work myself."

"Not too much trouble at all," Jules said. "Next time you come, we'll plug it into the amp and hear how it sounds. If you're interested in learning how to do some of the work, we'll start with the frets and the neck, but you might decide to do more down the road." He handed the guitar to Troy, "Take good care of her, there's a lot of wonderful music still to come from this instrument."

While Troy closed the latches on the case, Jules walked to the row of windows, his eyes on the sunlight that filtered through the lower branches of a maple tree. “I want to give you something to think about, reflect on, and even bring into your meditation practice until we see each other next.” He glanced at Troy, “Are you ready?”

Troy snapped the final latch closed and turned to face Jules, “You bet.”

“By not seeing the true nature of all phenomenon—which includes ourselves—we experience suffering. The potential to realize the freedom of our being is within us and has always been there. To experience that freedom, we need to first understand how to develop our minds and then actually reach a point in our practice where our true nature is revealed. Compassion and wisdom are considered the two wings of enlightenment. And like a bird needs two wings in order to fly, we must cultivate the two wings of compassion and wisdom to move us toward discovering our true nature and to eventually reach enlightenment. It takes time, Troy. It takes time, effort, and patience.”

“The way I look at it, Jules, time is going to pass one way or another. At the end of five years or fifty years or more, I can either come up empty handed or having gained something along the way. I’d rather do what I can to not come up empty handed.”

"Well, there's some wisdom right there," Jules smiled. "When can you come back so we can talk more?"

"Since I'm not taking any classes this summer, my afternoons are basically free toward the end of the day."

"How's next Wednesday, then? Four o'clock?"

"I'll be here. Is there anything I should bring?"

"If you want, you can bring your guitar. But otherwise," Jules pressed his hand on Troy's shoulder, "just bring an alert and open mind."

"You got it."

~

The supports when working for the sake of living beings
Are aspiration, steadfastness, joy and rest.
Aspiration is developed through fear of misery
And by contemplating the benefits of (aspiration) itself.
VII. 31

"Mom?"

"Hi, honey, I'm glad you're here," Rita called from the kitchen.

"What's up?" he asked, noticing her wiping her eyes and making an effort to form a smile that wouldn't quite form.

"I just got a call from Michelle. She said Uncle Jonathan fell last week, broke his hip, and now he's very sick with pneumonia. It doesn't sound good." Tears spilled from her eyes, and she strained to hold her voice steady, "I need to be there for him, and for her. It wasn't that long ago when Michelle lost her mother and now she's facing losing her father. They were all so good to me when my parents died; I just want to do whatever I can to be there for them."

"I'll call Theo and ask him to take me off the schedule for a couple of days. He'll understand. I'll try to line up someone to cover for me, and I'll drive you to see him," Troy put his arm around his mother's shoulders.

"I just started my new position at work, Troy. I don't know if they'll put up with me taking time off already."

"Mom, it's not like they don't know you. You've been working there for years; they know you're reliable. That's why they gave you the promotion. This is kind of an emergency. Uncle Jonathan is family. It'll be okay. We can drive down in the morning, and you'll only miss two days. We'll come back Sunday, and you'll be at work again Monday morning." Certainly he had seen his mother broken hearted before, but it had been when he was younger and was powerless to help her. This felt different, her heart was breaking again and he wanted her to know that this time she wouldn't have to face it alone. "Besides, Mom, it's not like they won't be able to reach you if they need to."

"You're right," she said. "I'll call the administrator now," she went to get her phone from her purse, pulling one thing after another from the large leather bag, piling her wallet, cosmetic bag, notebook, papers, and keys onto the kitchen table, "Ugh, where the hell is my phone?"

"Maybe you left it in the car, I'll go look," Troy took her keys from the table and ran outside, letting the screen door slam harder behind him than he'd expected. He found her phone resting on the console of her car and brought it inside. "I've got it, Mom; here you go."

"Thank you, honey," Rita held the phone, her hands shaking as she began to enter the number and then she stopped, closed her eyes, took a deep breath, and began again.

Troy listened as his mother explained the circumstances to her boss. He noticed the control in her voice as she apologized for the inconvenience and offered reassurance that she would be available by phone. Why, he wondered, does she feel that being gone for two days in order to be present for someone she loves and who is dying requires an apology? And, as he heard her express her concern for the people she works with and the nursing home residents she cares for, he saw the irony of his mother's small and fragile appearance that, from his more adult perspective, was an under-representation of her strength and courage. Was anyone more fiercely in his corner than her, even when he hadn't permitted her to be? How had he not seen this before?

"My son and I will be driving back Sunday, so I'll be in the office Monday," Rita explained to the person on the other end of the phone. "Of course, yes, if anything changes, I'll let you know." She wiped her eyes and looked up at the ceiling as if her tears could simply roll back where they came from. "Thank you, Viv, I appreciate that. Okay, then, see you soon. Goodbye."

"You were right, Troy. She couldn't have been nicer about it."

"Okay, well, is there anything we need to do before we go? Do you need anything? I can run to the store for you, or anything at all. I told Maggie I'd take her to dinner tonight, do you want to come with us?"

"Um, no, Troy. I'd like to stay here; the quiet helps me. Besides, I need to make a reservation at the hotel, pack a few things, and then get to bed early so we can get an early start in the morning." She gently rubbed her forehead, her fingers lightly sliding back and forth as if they were reading braille. "You can take my car when you go to dinner and fill it with gas, check the tires and oil and stuff like that."

"Okay, sure, I'll do that." He glanced at the clock on the wall, "I better get going then. What time do you want to be on the road?"

"I'd like to be on our way by six. It's about a five-hour drive, so that should get us there before noon."

"Okay," he said, "I'll be back early."

"Thanks, honey. I know this isn't quite the road trip you and I had in mind, but it'll help a lot to have you with me. I'll text Michelle and let her know we'll be there tomorrow."

"And Mom, don't convince yourself he won't get better," Troy said. "He might surprise everyone."

"That's a good thought. Okay, I'll hold onto that one. Thanks, honey."

~

Having forsaken all transgression, there would be no suffering,
And due to wisdom, there would be no lack of joy;
But now my mind is afflicted by mistaken conceptions
And my body is caused harm by unwholesome deeds.

As their bodies are happy due to their merits,
And their minds are happy due to their wisdom,
Even if they remained in cyclic existence for the sake of others,
Why would the Compassionate Ones ever be upset?
VII. 27, 28

After looking over the menu, Maggie said, "I'll have the Jungle Curry, but without fish sauce. Do you want to share an order of spring rolls or maybe some edamame?"

"Let's get both," Troy said. "The tofu with yellow noodles in red curry sauce looks good."

"Tofu?" she asked. "Seriously? You?"

Troy laughed, "Maybe you're just getting to me, Mags. I'm actually starting to like it." What he didn't say, just in case it was only a passing phase, was that he'd begun noticing that meat was becoming less appealing. He wasn't sure if it was Maggie's influence or the dharma, or a combination of the two.

After the waiter had taken their orders, they poured tea from the pot he had placed on the table and sipped green tea while they caught up on the day.

"I'm really sorry about your uncle, Troy. But I'm glad you can be there for your mom," Maggie took his hand in hers. "I'm going to miss you though. I mean, I know it's only a couple of days, and it's totally crazy, but still, I'll miss you. This is the first time either one of us will have been away since we met."

"Wow, that's right. I'll miss you too, Mags."

"I'll have a good distraction though," Maggie said. "I'm going to Mrs. Sternau's. I forgot to tell you that when I saw her on Thursday she said I could go there after work this weekend to paint."

"Excellent!" Troy said. "You can use the easel Abe gave you."

"That was the inspiration, Troy. I'm really looking forward to going. Hopefully the weather cooperates."

The waiter brought the appetizers to the table, and, as Maggie reached for a spring roll, she let her hand fall with a thud against the table, "Oh my god, I can't believe I forgot to ask you; how was your meeting with Abe's friend?"

"It was actually wonderful. But so much has happened today that it already feels like it was at least two days ago." He drizzled some peanut sauce on his spring roll. "Jules' shop is in a really sweet spot in the woods, and he's set up to do pretty much everything; he builds and repairs cellos, violins and acoustic guitars. He works on electric guitars and even has a couple of banjos hanging on his wall."

"Well, but what about teaching you? You know, about the dharma you want to study?"

"Oh, yeah, definitely. He gave me things to contemplate and to work into my meditation practice. Considering I wasn't there all that long, we covered a lot. He's pretty intense though. He doesn't waste time with chitchat, Maggie. He's all about the dharma no matter what he's doing, and he was really clear that I shouldn't be wasting time either. None of us should for that matter. He drove the point home that life is precious and every moment is essentially an opportunity to create something of value, and if we don't—or even worse, if our time is spent doing things that bring harm in any form—then we've missed an opportunity to do good for ourselves and others."

The waiter brought their meals to the table. They thanked him and arranged their dishes while Troy continued telling Maggie about Jules.

"Before I left, he told me it's really important to develop both compassion and wisdom; that they function like the two wings of a bird. In other words, you get nowhere with just one or the other, you need both working together."

"That makes sense," Maggie said. "But back-up a minute. I want to talk about that how-we-use-our-time thing. I mean life is crazy busy; everyone lives a ridiculously fast-paced existence. I think time is just an out-of-control element."

"Is it time that's out of control, Mags, or is it us? We're lucky enough to live someplace where we're not running for our lives. And so, I think we actually do have a choice in how we spend our time."

"Maybe we are running for our lives, Troy, and we just don't realize it."

Troy thought about what Maggie said for a moment, "If that's the case, Mags, then it's even more important that we know what direction we're running."

"Well, how would we know if we're running in the right direction or not?"

"When I was working with Abe, he told me about the ten non-virtuous actions and their reverse list that is the virtuous ones. So, you always want to be hovering around in the virtuous side of the equation."

"Okay," Maggie said, slowly working her chopsticks to pull a bamboo shoot from her plate. "The word 'virtuous' sounds so um, so biblical. So, what's on that list?"

"I was afraid you'd ask!" Troy answered. "Okay, I'll try. But first, when you hear a word like 'virtuous' you have to remember these concepts taught in the dharma don't have their origins in the English language. So, sometimes the word might sound weird to us but after a while you kind of stretch your understanding of the word to fit the context a little better. So, back to virtuous actions; you know the numbered lists in Buddhism are endless, right? No matter what, there is always a way to break something down into smaller and smaller parts."

"Yeah, you've told me about that. I think those lists are intimidating. I give you a lot of credit for trying to learn them," Maggie said, putting a few pieces of eggplant and mushrooms from her plate onto Troy's.

"Thanks, Mags. Do you want to try some of my tofu?"

"No, that's okay. Fish sauce, remember?" she said.

"Oh, sorry. I didn't realize it's in this too.

"Okay, so here's the list as best I remember it. I review this list pretty often in my meditations so they'll seep into my daily life. Then as things come up they're kind of running in the background and help steer me in the right direction. So, this'll be a good test for me to see if I've actually learned anything! Here it goes: There are three categories of actions in the list—actions of body, actions of speech, and actions of mind. In the body category the non-virtuous actions, the ones you definitely do not want to do because they're destructive and hurtful to others and also because they have negative karmic results for yourself, are killing, stealing, and wrong sex. Killing and stealing are pretty clear and obvious. The wrong sex part should be obvious too but it seems there are a lot of people who miss the obvious so we'll chalk that up to ignorance, which I'll come back to in a minute. Wrong sex includes things like rape or sex that involves any kind of deceit or abuse; incest, greed, infidelity, and things like that. You've got to remember that at the root of what distinguishes something between virtuous and non-virtuous is if the action brings harm to any sentient being, including yourself. And it's important to remember that all our actions, whether virtuous or not, will always deliver a similar result to whatever the action was. Like a seed just planted, once an action is taken, that seed over time will eventually grow into a large plant. This is how all things in life come about and develop—all actions we take as we interact with life around us are the causes, and the results of those actions are the effects. And that's why developing virtuous actions is so important. They become the antidotes to our non-virtuous actions. The more we do them, the more they become like a good habit that creates the sort of causes that will eventually bring good results. Since karma is guaranteed to multiply, then these good karmic results will multiply too. Does that make sense?" He paused, but not long enough for Maggie to respond. "You can think of the multiplying part like a seed that grows into a fully grown plant that bears lots of fruit. And I suppose that just like each piece of fruit contains more seeds, karmic results will always be more potent than the original action that caused them. Basically, it's at the heart of how all things exist in the on-going process of cause and effect, or 'the law of karma.'"

"Those non virtuous actions all seem like they should be easy enough to avoid, Troy."

"Maybe," he said. "But even if you yourself don't do one of those things, if you cause someone else to do them, then the resulting karma you've created is compounded by the fact that now you're responsible for someone else having taken on negative karma. For instance, let's say you've got cockroaches in your house and you hire an exterminator to get rid of them. The plot thickens, right? It's like you've hired a hit-man and now you've caused someone else to kill, and because you were the one that made the plan to do it, you've created killing karma."

"Oh, good Lord, that sounds pretty extreme. But, okay. And can we please not talk about cockroaches while we're eating?"

"Oh, sorry," Troy laughed. "Okay, but the rule of thumb is not to do harmful actions yourself, not to cause someone else to do them, and not to be happy about it when in either case the action has been taken. That's the moment-by-moment antidote to non-virtuous actions I was just talking about.

"So, moving on, next are the non-virtuous actions of speech. They're lying, divisive speech—in other words, saying things with the motivation of wanting to pit people against each other or to create divisions within groups of people or friends—and offensive speech, like speaking harshly toward someone, which of course is hurtful. And then there's idle speech, gossip, or sometimes it's just called senseless speech, which is the sort of conversation most of us are having way too much of!"

"So, what are you supposed to do when you run into someone and they want to just have a conversation like 'how-are-you' and 'what-have-you-been-up-to?"

"You can still be polite, I think you just try to keep meaningless conversation brief, that's all. And if they start gossiping about someone else you have to try your best to steer the conversation away from that. Not only for yourself, but for their karma too. And I think there are many skillful ways to steer idle conversations into meaningful ones. We just have to be mindful when we find ourselves in idle talk to do so. I've observed Grace and Abe do this. And even Jules, just in the one conversation we've had. It's actually very refreshing."

"It's an awful lot of rules, Troy."

"I know it seems that way, but if you think it through and begin to really understand the thing about karma because you've actually begun to observe it in action and you recognize how it works, it all becomes just a matter of common sense. And your natural impulse will be to do virtuous actions because they benefit everyone."

"Maybe," Maggie said with a hint of doubt. "But, go on. Is that it for speech? What's the next one?"

"Next are the actions of mind. Because it all starts there, right? Even if they're reflexive, any action you take is going to have its origins in your mind, so the non-virtuous states of mind are coveting, malice, and ignorance."

"Why ignorance?" Maggie asked. "I understand why no one would want to be ignorant, but I don't understand why it's on the non-virtuous list."

"Well, that's why I said we'd be coming back to it. Think about it, Mags. The crappy things people do are totally based on ignorance. For instance, something like fracking that uses enormous amounts of water and chemicals to blast through shale rock to get natural gas. Think about the harm that's done along the way to animals and people, and by contaminating the water which every living thing on the planet needs. It's like a domino effect of plants, animals, and humans being harmed or killed. Just think about where the killing, and in many cases, even the stealing karma falls as a result. Another example of ignorance is when people allow their minds to be filled with hate or self-righteousness, and on this basis think it's okay to kill or mistreat groups of people based on their religion, ancestry, gender, or ethnicity. Ignorance is a blatant misunderstanding of the true nature of all things—it's like going through life as if it's a game of blind-man's bluff. Anyway, do you get the idea how none of the non-virtuous things could possibly happen if there were no ignorance?"

"Yeah, I do." Maggie said. "That actually makes a lot of sense. But ignorance must be a tough one to get rid of, isn't it? I mean, think about it, it's everywhere. Everyone's pretty well convinced they're right even when they're clearly doing things on that harmful list."

"Exactly, Mags. That's why the two wings are so important: compassion and wisdom. If we have compassion we'll be patient and kind, right? And if we have wisdom, since we see things clearly, we'll know the right way to go about doing things. It's like these two wings are the antidotes to the things that cause all our trouble— compassion smothers selfishness, and wisdom crushes ignorance. As far as I can tell, it's the only way to live life, and in my opinion, the only shot we have at world peace."

~

When my strength declines, I should leave whatever I am doing
In order to be able to continue with it later.
Having done something well, I should put it aside
With the wish (to accomplish) what will follow.

VII. 67

"Troy, it's time to get up," Rita's voice startled Troy from a deep sleep.

"What time is it?" he asked.

"It's five," she said. "You have time for a shower; I'll make some breakfast."

The smell of coffee drew him out of bed and into the kitchen where Rita was making breakfast. "I'm not hungry, Mom. Don't make anything for me, okay?"

"Okay," she said, "but I'll pack a blueberry muffin so you can have it later if you want."

Troy was frustrated that he hadn't gotten up in time to do his meditation practice. So, he tried something else instead. He had read that a good practice to help strengthen mindfulness is to use the senses to bring awareness to the union of body and mind. Over time, this trains the mind to be thoroughly in tune with the body's experience. He held his mind's focus as best he could to be deeply present with his every step and action while he showered, shaved, and dressed for the drive. It is said that experiencing each moment in this way sharpens colors, textures, sounds, scents, and sensations, which in turn sharpen the mind's perceptions into a clearer state. This clearer state makes it possible to more confidently and skillfully direct all actions with archer-like precision.

He filled a knapsack with clothes and other things he would need for the two days he would be away, including some books and a notebook. As he thoughtfully chose the books he would take, he smiled at the difference between now and when he was in college and would have more likely been putting a six-pack of beer or a bong into his backpack than books. *Impermanence*, he thought to himself, *can be a beautiful thing.*

"I'll drive as far as Milford, Troy, and then you can drive the rest of the way. How's that sound?" Rita asked as they carried their bags and coffee mugs to the car.

"That'll work," he said. When he walked by the stream he noticed it was low from several days without rain. He thought of his plants, "Mom, sorry, but I've got to water everything out back before we go. It'll just take a minute." He turned on the faucet and dragged the hose around to the back of the cottage to give everything a good soaking, including the plant on his porch that Natalie and Maureen had given him. The morning air smelled of summer earth and moss, and grey clouds floated like drifting puzzle pieces in the sky. Troy found it poignant that in the same moments Uncle Jonathan could be approaching the end of his life, the earth simply carried on with its usual turnings, never skipping a beat. And that really, each moment is a continuous sequence of life's comings and goings. All the more reason to heed the advice he had heard from Jules the day before: that life is precious, and don't waste a second of it. Even in the mundane actions of watering plants or driving to Pennsylvania with his mother, with the right motivation and way of being present, every moment can be made sacred. He knew he had a lot to learn and practice before he could gain the mastery to really do this, but with people like Jules, Abe, Mrs. Sternau, and Grace to inspire him, it was an intriguing thought to consider as he turned off the faucet and walked back to join his mother.

Rita was already in the car with the engine running, all the windows down, sipping her coffee, and reviewing the map while she waited for Troy.

"I've got navigation on my phone, Mom, you don't need the map," Troy said as he climbed into the car and slid the passenger seat back as far as it could go.

"I like to know where I'm going," she said continuing to check her route before setting off. "I've heard those navigation things don't always give you the best route. I just don't trust them. Besides, I think it's dangerous the way people are so blindly dependent on all these new gadgets. Here, can you put this in the back seat?" Rita handed Troy the map and rolled slowly from the driveway toward the road. Traffic was already building for the morning commute as they approached the highway. "Damn it, I thought we'd beat the traffic."

"It'll thin out before too long," Troy said. "We've got about twenty miles of this, and then we should be good to go."

"I just hope Uncle Jonathan's going to be okay. I hate the thought of him suffering in a hospital bed with all those tubes and who knows what else," she said. "Maybe it was a mistake to leave this morning. Maybe we should've left last night. Oh my God, what if he dies before we get there?"

"I know. I don't like any of this either," Troy said. "But your worrying doesn't help, Mom. We didn't leave last night, we left when we left, and while most things are out of our control, worrying isn't one of them." Trying to be helpful he paraphrased a passage from Master Shantideva's *Guide to the Bodhisattva's Way of Life*[4], "I've read that worrying is basically useless because if there's something you can do about a situation then you'll do it, so there's no need to worry. And then—if there's nothing that can be done, well, there's nothing you can do so worrying is useless then too."

"Yeah, well, maybe that's true but it's not working on me. I'll think about it another time when I'm not so busy worrying, okay?"

He realized that any further effort to interrupt his mother's angst at this point would only backfire. So, they drove in silence instead, Rita's white Nissan just one of what seemed to be an endless stream of cars and trucks, all traveling one direction or another in more of life's comings and goings. Eventually the traffic thinned as the highway took them past hills covered with pine

4 Chapter VI v 10

and birch trees, modest box-shaped houses that dotted the landscape here and there, and small lakes and ponds that offered pink tinged grey and white clouds back to the morning sky.

Finally, when they reached the exit for Milford, Rita suggested they stop and stretch their legs. "Let's go to the restaurant across the street from that old brick church." Waiting for the light at the end of the ramp, she looked at Troy and asked, "Are you hungry? You don't have to eat that muffin if you'd rather have something else. We can both get something to go." She laughed, "True confession—I just want to use their restroom, and it feels too conspicuous and rude to not buy something."

"Okay. I am starting to get a little hungry. I'll see what they've got; I could go for a grilled cheese with tomato."

"That sounds good. Will you order one for me too?"

"Sure, Mom."

~

Without indulging in despondency, I should gather the supports (for enthusiasm)

And earnestly take control of myself.
(Then by seeing) the equality between self and others,
I should practice exchanging self for others.
VII. 16

The Pennsylvania landscape looked much the way Troy had remembered it. Old stone farmhouses; stretches of fields with neat green rows of corn reaching yardstick-straight toward the sky; barns and silos; and pastures where cows, unaware of their fate, were patiently swinging their tails and twitching flies from their backs.

"Oh! Here's a text from Michelle." Rita read the message to Troy: "Dad's out of the ICU. He's still weak. Mostly sleeping but he's opened his eyes and been talking. The nurses say that's a good sign. I told him you're on your way. He smiled. Can't wait to see you both."

"We're getting close, Mom. There're the signs for the hospital."

Rita exhaled a long sigh, closed her eyes and said, "I'm not so big on prayer, but if I were to give it a shot, I'd start praying for strength right about now. I don't want to fall apart when I see him."

"Mom, you're one of the strongest people I know. But if you cry, you cry. I think that's okay."

"If I start to cry, the hard part is stopping the crying. He doesn't need me showing up at his bedside and dissolving into tears."

"So, do you want to try something that might help?" Troy asked.

"Sure, but what? Are you going to tell me not to worry again?"

"No, Mom. First, try to relax your defensiveness just a bit, okay? Can you do that?"

"Okay, sure. I'm sorry."

"Well, first you need to sit straight," he glanced at his mom and watched her straighten her back against the seat. "Then it's probably easiest if you close your eyes and just take a few breaths. Just normal, gentle breaths, Mom." He waited for her to get situated with her breathing. "Then try to imagine your breath like it's something you can actually watch coming into your body, maybe even filling your whole body instead of just your lungs and then watch it leave again. Do that a bunch of times." He waited quietly for her to establish a calm, steady rhythm of breath.

"Now imagine the thing you'd most like to do for Uncle Jonathan. Like, doing whatever you can to relieve any pain or fear he's experiencing." Again, he waited for her to form her own thoughts. "Now, imagine that as you're breathing in, you're also taking away all his pain and fear. Then as you breathe out, imagine that you're giving him peace, comfort, and love." Troy stopped talking, and as he followed the signs to the hospital, he felt his words grounding his own mind into a similar space he was guiding his mother toward. The two sat quietly as he drove. When he finally reached the stoplight in front of the hospital's visitor parking, his mother opened her eyes.

"Wow, Troy," she said softly, "That really helped. I mean it totally took all those sharp edges away for me. I might actually be able to do this now. It's not going to be easy, but I do feel a little stronger, and more calm."

Troy smiled and said, "The cool thing, Mom, is that you can do this again anytime you need. Now that you know the steps, you can walk yourself through them quickly if you only have a minute, or you can spend more time with them when you have the time."

"Thank you, honey," she said as she pulled a brush through her thick hair and bunched it with a clip into a loose bun. She pulled the visor down to use the mirror, quickly slid a berry shade of lipstick along her lips and tossed it along with her brush back into her purse. As she pushed the visor back up and opened her door, she turned to look at Troy and said, "I'm getting the distinct feeling that you've learned a lot since you've come back home. It's funny how life works that way, isn't it? I mean, you went to college to learn things like political science, business, or whatever and with all the unexpected and painful things that happened, you ended up learning more about life than anything else." She smiled and added, "It's incredibly fulfilling for me as your mom to realize that you have so much to teach me. I'm proud of you, Troy. Truly. Things could've persisted in a downward spiral for you, but you've taken your difficulties and used them to make yourself wiser and stronger. I couldn't be happier."

"Thanks, Mom. That's really good to hear. I've watched you bounce back from a lot, too. Maybe it's rubbed off on me."

Rita laughed, "Well, there certainly is a lot of bouncing that goes on in this crazy life."

~

Even doctors eliminate illness
With unpleasant medical treatments,

So in order to overcome manifold sufferings
I should be able to put up with some discomfort.

Yet the Supreme Physician does not employ
Common medical treatments such as these,
With an extremely gentle technique,
He remedies all the greatest ills.
VII. 23, 24

They walked together to the hospital entrance, each preparing in their own way for how it might be to see Jonathan. At the front desk in the lobby, the woman behind the desk looked in the directory and told Rita and Troy he was on the sixth floor, in room number 635. They waited for the elevator in the hallway and watched the lights on the wall track the elevators' descents and ascents—more comings and goings, Troy thought. He also thought about birth and death, and that here in the hospital, both were condensed within an environment of electronic sounds and soft voices as people talked quietly or not at all, withdrawn into their own experience of life's most intense moments. The elevator doors slid open, and a small woman with dark hair pushed a cleaning cart as she left the elevator along with two doctors in white jackets. They walked around the corner, going from one level to another in a well-traveled maze they knew like the back of their hands. Troy held his hand against the open door and waited for his mother, and then for a young couple that came running to catch the elevator before he stepped in to join them. Rita pressed the button for the sixth floor, and the other man reached to press the ninth. Everyone's eyes were directed somewhere other than at each other as the elevator jerked upward and they rode in silence to the sixth floor.

The signs on the wall directed them to the right. Troy rested his hand lightly on his mother's shoulder as they walked past the nurses' desk toward Jonathan's room.

"Here it is," Rita whispered to Troy. They stood outside the door as if they were waiting for their hearts to catch up with their bodies—or maybe it was the other way around. Regardless, it was a gathering of sorts, a gathering of strength and love before stepping into the room. A curtain was drawn around the bed and a nurse came through the doorway behind them and spoke softly, "It'll be a few minutes before he's ready. They're cleaning him and checking his vitals now. His daughter is waiting down the hall for you and asked me to let you know she's there."

"Oh, thank you," Rita said.

"Follow me," the nurse said. "I'll show you where she is."

She led them to the end of the corridor where several chairs and end tables were arranged in living room fashion. There was no soft upholstery on the chairs; all surfaces were shiny and stiff with chrome edges and mango-colored vinyl seats. Facing a row of windows, Michelle was standing silhouetted against the bright sunlight that spilled through the glass.

"Ma'am," the nurse said, "your visitors are here."

Michelle turned just as Rita and Troy were approaching her. It had been a year or two since she and Rita had seen each other and even longer since she had seen Troy. Hugs were exchanged all around with smiles and tears as Michelle thanked them for coming to see her father and told them that she felt he was actually doing better today than he had been the day before. "I've not given up hope," she said. "He's going to be so happy to see you both. I know your being here will make his day."

It was only a few minutes later that the nurse returned. "You can go in anytime you're ready."

"How was the drive?" Michelle asked as they walked toward her father's room.

"It wasn't bad," Rita said. "Troy did most of the driving."

"Troy, it's been so long since I've seen you. You're all grown now. How did that happen in such a hurry?"

"I don't know," Troy laughed. "It hasn't always felt like it's been in such a hurry to me."

"Oh, I can appreciate that," Michelle said.

Michelle led the way into her father's room. She gently placed her hand on his shoulder and said, "Dad, look who's here!"

Jonathan turned to look toward the door. "Wonderful." His voice was weak. His eyes followed Rita and Troy as they walked to gather around his bed. "As if the sun doesn't make enough light of its own," he paused to catch his breath, "you're like a couple of portable suns."

Rita leaned carefully around the IV tubes and the oxygen catheter in his nose, and kissed him lightly on his cheek just above a coarse, silvery growth of beard. "It's so good to see you, Jonathan. When Michelle told me what happened I couldn't wait to get here, and thankfully Troy was able to take off from work to come with me."

Troy wasn't sure what to do. Should he hug him, or shake his hand? The IVs made the whole situation awkward so he just reached to take his uncle's hand and held it. "Hi Uncle Jonathan. Michelle says you're doing a little better today; they must be taking good care of you." He looked at the arrangement of tubes delivering various things. "It's a pretty intricate set-up you've got going on here."

"Yes, indeed," he smiled weakly. Jonathan's hand felt cool as he very lightly squeezed Troy's hand. "Thank you for coming."

"He's lost some weight, but look—there's some pink in his cheeks," Michelle said, stroking her father's hair, smoothing some of the strands into a semblance of having been combed. "Don't try to talk, Daddy, there will be time for that when you're feeling a little stronger, okay? You rest, and I'll tell Rita and Troy what's been going on."

Jonathan nodded and closed his eyes as Michelle took his hand in hers.

"They've put a pin in his hip and while that's mending okay, it's the pneumonia that's been the real complication. Thankfully he was in pretty good shape before he fell, so that's given him a fighting chance. He spiked a fever, but thank God they started the antibiotics quickly because they're helping. The doctor said he's begun to need a little less oxygen. He still doesn't have much appetite, but he'll try some broth at lunch." She turned her attention to her father again, "You'll need to drink that broth, Dad. It'll help you get your strength back." He nodded weakly. His eyes were heavy with fatigue as he took in the faces gathered around him and then gently closed his eyes again.

Michelle bit her lip as she fought tears that welled in her eyes from both exhaustion and worry; the dark circles beneath her eyes appeared like bruises against the paleness of her skin. "They want him up and moving as soon as possible. They've been doing what they can to help by moving him in his bed to prevent bedsores, but now he needs to be able to get up in order for that hip to heal."

Troy stood on the opposite side of the bed from Michelle while she and Rita spoke quietly to each other, catching up on things that had been going on since they were last together. Troy thought about karma's ongoing ripening as he observed its unfolding at Jonathan's bedside. He thought about how karma is connected to everything, including the way all bodies reach their natural expiration point. Mrs. Sternau said that death was like slipping into another day carrying the karmic accumulations of the day before. She said you could think of it like continuing energy, or maybe like a bundle of DNA loaded with ingredients you've put into it over countless lifetimes. She explained that its pattern—or karma—manifests as it moves along with the being from one lifetime into the next. There was so much she had said that day that now felt distant and a little less clear to Troy. But this particular conversation held important threads that he wanted to pick up with Jules. He could see there is a path to follow and that it is well marked, but you'll only recognize those markings if you've learned what to look for. That can't happen without the help of a good teacher.

Michelle checked her watch, "It's almost noon; I didn't even think to ask if you'd had lunch before you got here. Are you hungry? There's a cafeteria downstairs."

"We stopped for something to eat on our way," Rita said. "I don't know about Troy, but I'm not hungry. We'll join you though if you'd like to get something."

"Sure, I'd like that," Michelle said. "But maybe we should wait until after they've brought his lunch. I want to be sure he drinks the broth and encourage him to eat something more."

"You guys go ahead," Troy said. "I'll sit here with Uncle Jonathan and read until they bring his lunch. I can text you when his lunch gets here."

"That's a good idea," Rita said. "I might head over to the hotel to check in."

"Are you sure you wouldn't rather stay at my house?" Michelle asked. "It's only about ten miles from here."

"Thanks, Michelle, that's really nice of you to offer, but staying at the hotel will be easier. It's just up the road. Besides, if I were in your shoes the last thing I'd want to be doing is hosting houseguests."

"Well, when you come next time, consider it an open invitation." She leaned to kiss her father's forehead. "Daddy, Rita and I will be back soon; Troy's going to stay here while we get some lunch."

~

Troy heard their voices fade as Michelle and his mother walked down the corridor, then the chime of the elevator, and the low hum of the doors sliding open and closed. He reached for his backpack and slowly pulled the zipper, trying to open it as quietly as possible. He took one of the books from the pack and leafed through the pages to where he had left off several days earlier. Jonathan slept peacefully while medicines, oxygen, and fluids streamed a network of healing gently into his body. Troy found the page he was looking for and re-read a few paragraphs to reorient to the topic being discussed. He found the material demanded quite a bit of effort to comprehend, but what he lacked in academic training, he made up for in curiosity and determination.

"What are you reading?" Jonathan asked, his raspy voice startling Troy from his absorption in the book.

"Oh, hey, Uncle Jonathan, I hope I didn't wake you up. It's a book by the Dalai Lama."

"I hear he's a good man. Read something to me."

"Um, sure, let me find a good spot to start from," Troy said.

"Just start where you are."

"Okay, but just a heads-up—it's not exactly light reading."

"It'll be good for my brain."

Troy skimmed the first few paragraphs on the page the book was opened to and started at the bottom of the page. "'Buddhism teaches that everything arises from causes and conditions and that therefore there is no such thing as an uncaused cause. If there were such a thing, then everything could be said to arise from nothing! Alternatively, the primal substance would have to be constantly giving rise to (causing) something. But as we can see, phenomena sometimes manifest and at other times do not. This is because the causes and conditions on which they depend sometimes come together and at other times do not.

"'If the cause were independent and able to create constantly, then of course its results would also have to be constant. Since the results are not constant, we can argue that their cause also is not constant; it is impermanent...[5]'"

"Lunch is here," a man said, carrying a tray into the room from the cart he had left outside the door. He pushed a box of tissues out of the way to clear space for the tray on the table. "The nurse will be coming in a few minutes to help," he said on his way back out.

"What've we got there?" Jonathan asked after the man left the room.

Troy stood to look at the items on the tray, there weren't many. "It looks like a bowl of broth, a container

---

5 For the Benefit of All Beings, A Commentary on the Way of the Bodhisattva, by His Holiness the Dalai Lama, Shambhala, 2009

of yogurt, and a container of Jell-O. Oh, there's a glass of apple juice, too."

His expression soured. "I guess if I want to understand what you just read, I'll need strength, so I'll eat."

Troy laughed, "I know what you mean. Some of this makes my head spin. But I'm not supposed to be tiring you out, Uncle Jon; I'm supposed to be helping you rest. So, save your strength for getting better, okay? I'll read more another day if you want."

Jonathan just smiled and closed his eyes again, and Troy returned to his reading while they waited.

"Jonathan," a nurse with a strong voice came into the room. "I'm going to raise your bed and help you with your lunch."

Troy stood to get out of the way. She had a system for how to make everything happen with the least disruption, including a strategic placement of pillows to help prop Jonathan up to sit. She said the doctor said he was doing well enough that he could be taken off the oxygen while he ate. She helped him with the first few spoonsful of broth and then handed him the spoon to try it out on his own. His hand had a slight tremor that caused him to spill on the tray and the napkin the nurse had draped against his chest. After only three or four more spoonsful he said he was done. She coaxed him to try a few more and then encouraged him to try a few bites of the red Jell-O.

Troy texted his mother that Jonathan was eating and she responded right away that they were both elated and would be on their way back soon.

After he was finished, the nurse put the oxygen back under Jonathan's nose, and said she'd like him to stay upright for a little while before lowering the bed again. She checked all the monitors to the various things he was hooked up to around his bed and left the room saying she would check back in about ten minutes. "Push the button if you need help sooner," she said, and then turned to Troy and added, "He'll be very tired from all he's just done and so, right now, rest is extremely important. As long as he's kept very quiet, I'm sure it's comforting for him to have you here."

"Okay," Troy smiled, "I'll be quiet."

~

Before they left on Sunday morning, Troy and Rita said their goodbyes to Jonathan and Michelle at the hospital. Jonathan sat in a wheelchair while the nurses changed his bedding. He turned a major corner, they said, when he managed a few steps with a walker the day before, and he began breathing more on his own. Jonathan looked tired and not nearly as enthusiastic as everyone else was about his progress. Michelle explained that the plan was to get him up more throughout the day and then the next step would be to stabilize him and move him to a rehab facility for physical therapy.

Goodbyes are never easy, but with the hopefulness for a good recovery and Rita's promise to return in the next week or two, their hugs carried the assurance they'd be seeing each other again soon.

"Goodbye, Uncle Jonathan," Troy reached for his hand.

"Thanks for coming," Jonathan said. "Take good care of your mother."

Troy's throat tightened. Jonathan's words were a passing of the torch. "I'll do my best," he said. "I'll come back to see you soon."

"Bring that book with you when you come. We'll see if it makes any more sense to me then."

"You got it," Troy said. And with that, they were on their way.

~

"Compared to the prognosis of a few days ago, I think he's doing pretty well," Rita said as they wound their way back to the highway. "I really thought we were about to lose him."

"It was a close call, Mom, but do you really think he's out of the woods?" Troy didn't say what he was really thinking, which was that it was only a matter of time, and if not this time, it would probably be something else not that far in the future.

"I think he's got a good chance of bouncing back. He's begun to rebuild his strength and if he's got the determination to work hard through the physical therapy, that'll make a big difference. I think we can be hopeful."

~

The Mighty One himself has said
That aspiration is the root of every facet of virtue;
Its root is constant acquaintance
With the ripening-effects (of actions).
VII. 40

Wednesday afternoon, on his way to see Jules, Troy carried his guitar as far as the door, hesitated, and then decided to leave it behind. Of course, he wanted to begin replacing the frets and learning how it's done, but the experience with Jonathan had raised some haunting questions. As Troy saw it, exploring these questions with Jules had to be the priority.

Jules was standing at the end of the driveway taking mail from his mailbox when Troy turned onto Dogwood Lane.

"Greetings!" Jules said. "You came just in time to spare me from sorting through all this rubbish they call 'mail' these days." He lightly flipped through the envelopes, "Look at all these credit card offers; apparently this world wants me in debt." He laughed and shook his head. "Go ahead on in, I'll meet you in the studio."

"Okay." Troy rolled in just beyond reach of the black walnut tree that dropped nuts in lime-green husks, snapping twigs as they fell in thuds to the ground.

"Where's your guitar?" Jules asked.

"Oh, I left it at home," Troy answered, searching Jules' face for disappointment. It hadn't dawned on him that Jules might have had his mind set on the guitar. "A lot's happened since I saw you last. I didn't know how much time you'd have available today, so I thought focusing on the dharma would be a good move."

He told Jules about Jonathan, and the trip he and his mother had taken to visit him in the hospital. "You and I talked about having the good fortune to be born human and about making good use of the opportunities we have in life if we don't waste our time. Um—and I'm not saying working on guitars is a waste of time. It's just that I'd really like your help reconciling some things that just aren't adding up for me. Can I bring the guitar next time?"

"Sure. But in time you'll learn you can bring the dharma into any activity you're doing. We live a worldly life, but that doesn't mean your dharma practice can't be part of it. Then, as we go about living our worldly life, all is done with a real sense of joy."

"I'm glad to hear you say that. Is that something that can be taught, or is it something I need to figure out on my own?"

"A little of both, you'll see. But tell me, what's going on?"

"So, when we were on our way to see my uncle, based on what we had heard, my mom and I were preparing to lose him. We wanted to be a good presence for him, and also support his daughter who grew up like a sister to my mom. It turned out that the antibiotics they gave him kicked in and for now he's holding steady. But the whole experience felt like a fire drill, if you know what I mean. It made me think about things you'd said last time I was here—like how quickly life goes, how fragile we all are as we move through it, and how rare and precious it is to have a human life. As I sat in the room with my uncle, there seemed to be nothing of any real use that I could do to help him. Did he even want to talk about dying? And if he did, I didn't think I should be the one to bring it up. Death was the elephant in the room. No one really wants to talk about it, yet there it is, staring us all in the face from the moment we're born, right? I don't even know what I would have said anyway. But here's where I'm having a hard time accepting some of what we talked about last week; I think my uncle has lived a good life. I mean, he's lived well, worked hard, and raised a family. He's been a good husband and father, and on top of all that he's basically been generous and kind. A lot of people go through life that way, so how is that a problem? That story you told about the turtle and the yoke—do people like my uncle blow their chances at finding a human life again if they don't happen to stumble upon the dharma? And if so, why isn't living a good life like his enough?"

"First of all, I like to have tea in hand for conversations like this. Besides, it's 4:00—that means it's officially tea time."

"Well, back in the day, I would've said it was beer time. But I've put that habit to rest. Tea sounds good."

Jules laughed, "I've known a lot of people who needed to do exactly what you did. I think it's pretty impressive that you figured it out this early in life."

"Not to be dramatic, but it came down to choosing life or death, and in that light—even through some dark moments—for me, the decision was pretty clear."

Jules heated water on a hot plate that he kept in the corner of the studio. Next to it was a shelf that held a small stack of dishes, bowls, and mugs. Troy was intrigued by the efficient simplicity of everything about Jules. Nothing was overly elaborate, and nothing was lacking. Even in the way he lifted the mugs from the shelf and pulled tea bags from the black and gold tin, Jules moved in a steady tempo that beat a silent pulse.

"Is black tea okay with you?" Jules asked. "I've got herbal tea if you'd rather."

"No, black tea's fine," Troy said. "With sugar or honey if you have it."

Jules pulled a bowl of sugar from the shelf, and took a spoon from a jar that held a few utensils. "Sure, come fix it the way you like it."

They made their tea and pulled stools over to sit by the row of opened windows where they'd sat last time Troy visited. A breeze puffed the steam like a string of smoke signals from their tea.

Jules rested the cup on the workbench and cleared his throat before he spoke. "Karma isn't something that belongs to a religion, Troy. It's potential, if you will. The potential of our actions. So, whether someone connects with the dharma in their life or not, karma is always doing its thing, creating the potential of what's to come from our actions. The deal with the dharma is that it is a collection of flawless and powerful teachings, or guidance. And, along with the Four Noble Truths, you'll find that one of the most important foundational principles it teaches us about is karma, and a lot of detail about how it works. The dharma offers many methods to strategically navigate life in order to break free from the suffering that comes along with cyclic existence—in other words, 'samsara'— and it starts with a firm understanding of how life works for all beings in existence, directly as a result of karma. So, once you recognize karma is the potential of actions, generated by your own actions of body, speech, and mind that are creating a 'becoming' or 'potential,' you'll be very motivated to exercise wisdom in the way you live your life. But you need to understand that there's not some kind of jury out there when you die that's handing out pass or fail karma tickets. If you don't create a karma, it cannot ripen. Just like if you don't plant a seed, it will not grow. And even if you do plant a seed, it isn't until it meets the right conditions that it begins to take root and grow. There are detailed instructions in the dharma for how to create the best conditions for your good karma to flourish, how to eliminate the causes for creating negative karma, and as we talked about before, how to purify negative karma." He laughed and added, "Staying with the metaphor of planting seeds, we could think of the dharma like the ultimate farmer's almanac." Jules' dark eyes met with Troy's, "You're not born human because you've studied the dharma. You're born human because of your karma. Karma is the stored potential, residing in our most subtle mind. It's created by our actions, and once created, its imprints are carried with us from life to life, and will eventually ripen, moment-by-moment, as we live our life.

"Once we've been introduced to this particular wisdom the dharma offers, we come to know and value the opportunities of a human life in a very profound way. This creates a strong incentive to learn and practice what the dharma provides. And with the deeper understanding that comes as a result of studying and practicing the dharma, things like recognizing on a very deep level how karma works and the interdependence of absolutely everything that exists, we open different dimensions to the playing field that we ordinarily perceive and engage in as merely a three-dimensional experience of ordinary, daily life. This view allows for something alchemic, bordering on magical to happen when what we've previously known as a suffering existence becomes one of happiness and joy."

Troy frowned and combed his hand through his hair as if doing so would open his mind to a better understanding. "I get it—so that means everyone, my uncle included, is experiencing the results of their own karma. What I'm trying to do, Jules, is to absorb and apply all of this—not just by following rules of what to do and what not to do, but by managing my mind. Where do I start?"

"Great question," Jules said with a smile. "But I'd say you've already started. The better question might be, 'What now?'"

"Okay," Troy said. "What now?"

~

Due to the strength of the Awakening Mind,
The Bodhisattvas consume their previous transgressions
And Harvest oceans of merit:
Hence they are said to excel the Shravakas.
VII. 29

"First of all, every sentient being, from the smallest life form to the largest, has an immortal potency or element, something called Buddha Nature. This pure nature is the same as that of the buddhas and is the actual potential for every sentient being to attain Buddhahood, or enlightenment. We refer to this as 'abiding buddha nature.' This is a potential that must be nourished and cultivated in order for ultimate buddha nature to become functional. So, in order to do that we need to cultivate another type of buddha nature called 'developing buddha nature.' Because we can't just pull this sort of thing out of thin air—unless you're some extraordinary being who has already achieved extraordinary attainments in previous lives—we definitely need a teacher to present us with the appropriate instruction.

"So, under the guidance of a qualified teacher we need three things: to study the dharma, contemplate what we've studied, and engage in a meditation practice. Done together, study, contemplation, and meditation lead us to cultivate deeper levels of compassion and *bodhicitta*, which is the strong determination to achieve enlightenment for the sake of all sentient beings, a determination that springs from compassion and wisdom. I cannot emphasize the importance of meditation enough. So, get ready, because you'll hear me drive that point home over and over again. All that you're learning and attempting to put into practice is given strong roots through meditation. We all endure a lot of storms in life, and if you've grown your dharma practice so that it's deeply rooted in your mind, you'll weather those storms in direct proportion to the depth of the roots of your practice. If a tree doesn't have deep roots when a storm hits, it's easily uprooted after heavy rains and strong winds, right? That's what happens to us if we don't send the roots of our learning deep into our minds. Those roots are propelled by the strength of conviction. And true conviction can only come through unshakable knowledge and experiencing the truth of that knowledge. That's true wisdom. None of that can happen without a consistent meditation practice. I'm sure you know this already, but it's important to add that a successful meditation practice isn't left behind when you leave your cushion and walk into daily life."

"So, then, maybe that's what I should be asking for; guidance for a meditation practice."

"Sure, that's definitely a good start. But before we get to that I just want to plant a few ideas for you to think about and for you to hold in your mind."

"Okay," Troy said, adjusting his position on the stool, bracing his feet against the lower bar that secured its legs.

"Buddha nature, like space, is not produced by a cause. So, let's first talk about the mind. The mind is actually like a mirror. It only reflects any quality that appears to it. Hold that thought, and now understand that the mind's quality, like a mirror is that of emptiness."

"What do you mean, by the quality of emptiness?"

"That like everything else, the existence of the mind depends on causes and conditions; the mind doesn't simply exist in and of itself any more than your arm doesn't exist without things like cells, bones, muscles, nerves, and so on. In other words, it only exists in dependence upon a confluence of causes and conditions, and therefore has the quality of impermanence and change. This is why it's possible for your mind to be angry in one moment and loving in another, peaceful and calm in one moment and anxious in another, to change from a state of ignorance on a topic to one of being knowledgeable because it has the capacity to reflect, and to reflect upon what appears to it, like a mirror. It also has the capacity to transform suffering to happiness in dependence upon the positive or 'virtuous' actions that we take. So now, bringing this back to Buddha nature, the mind's quality of emptiness *is* Buddha nature. Emptiness itself is unchanging, however emptiness is the quality that allows the mind to change and that therefore makes it possible for all sentient beings to achieve Buddhahood."

Jules looked into his teacup and swirled his tea before finishing the last sip. "The Buddha who taught these teachings over 2500 years ago is known as

Shakyamuni Buddha. However, according to some texts, the number of buddhas is innumerable, and previous to each one having achieved Buddhahood there was an ordinary sentient being like you and me. Animals, insects, you name it; if it's sentient it has Buddha nature. But getting back to Shakyamuni Buddha, it was he, who having achieved enlightenment—or Buddhahood—delivered the teachings of the dharma to humanity so that others could also pursue the path to be free from the sufferings of cyclic existence. This all starts with understanding the Four Noble Truths and how karma and emptiness work in dependence on our actions.

"We can think of the Buddha as a great doctor, ourselves and others as patients, and the Buddha's teachings as medicine. Just because we're not on our deathbed with an illness doesn't mean we're without dysfunctional conditions that disrupt our wellbeing. So, even if your body is strong as an ox, the ripening good karma continuously occurring in your mind is the source of your wellbeing. Shakyamuni Buddha was so skillful that he knew precisely how to deliver his teachings based on the capacity of those he was teaching and in such a way that they could understand. Like choosing the appropriate medicine and its dosage, he modified his teachings to suit the capacity of the student so that the student could benefit most from what he presented. And all these centuries later, it's been my observation that these methods still hold up.

"For some people, the most appropriate thing for them to learn is how to make their present life better. They're not concerned about future lives or nirvana or any such thing other than right now. Then, there are others who have an awareness of past and future lives, and because they also understand the function of karma, are concerned about increasing their odds for a better future life. For some, their goal is nirvana, which is a permanent state of wisdom and bliss, free from samsara. And finally, there are others who embrace all the practices that each of those types of people engage in but who have also realized a profound level of compassion and wisdom. This compels them to align with the goal of Buddhahood, or enlightenment with the intention to eliminate suffering for all sentient beings."

"Jules, sorry, I really don't mean to be disrespectful at all, but you said the number of buddhas is innumerable; if there are already so many buddhas, why are there still so many people suffering?"

"It's not disrespectful to question. You've got to question everything or those roots of learning will never do more than scratch the surface of your mind. Even if the greatest teachers on the planet tell you everything they know, until you convert what they've taught you into your own knowledge, it'll be gone with the first puff of wind. So, as I said before—listen, study, contemplate and meditate. Without all of those steps together, to only engage in one or two, borders on being a waste of time. If you want to make any progress on this path, there's no room for laziness. So, keep your skepticism while also keeping an open mind.

"Now, in response to your question. Buddhas, like doctors, don't run around tackling people and forcing the dharma down their throats. They reveal the dharma, they teach it to you, but you have to decide to turn to it for help. That's the silver lining of suffering existence. Ironically, it's through our experience of suffering that we are moved to turn toward something that will make it stop. So, although the Buddha's first Noble Truth seems very harsh, that the nature of existence is suffering, it is what actually moves us to find its cure. And the dharma is there as the exact medicine you need. 'Take as directed,' and you'll be free of suffering. And Troy, while you're not in this alone, the bottom line is you're the one that's in the driver's seat."

"What do you mean, 'you're not in it alone?' Who's in it with you?" Troy asked.

"Well, I've mentioned the Buddha as the teacher, and the dharma as the medicine. There's a third element that's called the sangha. The three together comprise what is called 'The Three Jewels.'"

"Sangha." Troy repeated the word, frustration seeping through his voice. "What's that?" He knew he'd heard the word when Abe had mentioned The Three Jewels once before, but at this point it was only vaguely in his memory like so many other terms and ideas he'd heard. It seemed every time he got his mind around one thing, something new was thrown into a floating collection of moving parts he wanted desperately to see as a complete picture.

"Sangha commonly refers to the community of monks and nuns, and others who have achieved high realizations. They're like traveling companions on the path who demonstrate the practice through their living example as well as by sharing teaching and guidance with people who want to learn."

"So, then, are you my sangha?"

"Technically, no. 'Dharma friend,' yes—'sangha,' no. Even for monks and nuns, a sangha isn't formed until there are four or more together. And I don't have the high realizations to qualify alone as sangha. However, if you stay with this as you're doing, putting effort into study and practice, you won't help but be able to make that connection because you're creating the conditions for that karma to ripen."

"You really think so?"

"I know so."

~

Likewise, I shall have to realize
Many excellent qualities for myself and others,
And (in order to attain) each of these qualities (alone)
I may have to acquaint myself with its cause until an ocean of aeons is exhausted.
VII. 35

"Are you familiar with The Three Poisons, Troy?"

"Yes, I am. It's another list, but at least it's a short one." Troy drummed on his knees, "They're ignorance, desire and anger, right?"

"You got it," Jules said. These are considered to be the root of all other mental afflictions. For instance, hatred is also a mental affliction and its root is anger. While anger is something that is current in the mind, hatred is something that seeps from past into present and future and therefore, because it is the spark for anger, is actually even more dangerous than anger. Another example is of desire being the root for attachment. Desire fuels attachment and attachment fuels desire and without wisdom, both create the potential for a lot of negative actions to follow. Bottom line, together with ignorance the three poisons are the underlying cause of everything we do that wreaks havoc in our lives. The Three Poisons are the root of what have been identified as 84,000 mental afflictions and they are also the root cause of negative karma. Don't ask me who counted them, but as there are 84,000 mental afflictions, there are in turn 84,000 antidotes offered by the Buddha's teaching." Jules paused as he saw an expression of overwhelm cloud Troy's face. "Don't worry," he added, "we're not going through each of them. This is why we focus on the Three Poisons, because if we can tackle them then we can skillfully eliminate all 84,000. I just want you to understand that regardless of their number, although they're often so subtle they're hard to recognize, they're always with us in some way or another, and therefore extremely powerful in their destructive nature. I have this picture of them in my mind as if our entire body, all our senses, and our mind with all its predilections and perceptions are literally loaded with glowing embers of mental afflictions; like they're all little crumbs of fire and all it takes is one inflammatory splash of fuel—an offensive remark that is heard or read, an object either seen or touched—any of these can be like gas on fire, whether it's pride, covetous desire, jealousy, or whatever, it bursts into flames and consumes us, destroying our peace like a fast spreading fire."

"That's a pretty vivid description, Jules," Troy winced. "Um, I think I've personally had that experience more than a few times."

"Of course you have," Jules said. "Here you are, a human walking around on this planet. It's inevitable that you'd come fully equipped with mental afflictions included. Not only our own body, but the entirety of all existence can be seen like a composite of all 84,000 mental afflictions being ignited continually in the moment-by-moment of arising interactions with all sentient beings." He clasped his hands together behind his head, arching into a stretch against the back of the stool. "But remember what we were just saying about impermanence and emptiness?"

"Yeah."

"If it's possible for mental afflictions to wax and wane, to sometimes be present and other times not present at all, then it's possible for them to be reduced. And if they can be reduced, then it's also possible for them to be eliminated. Therefore, mental afflictions have all the ingredients of impermanence and like everything else, they are not inherently existent."

"But how do you ever truly get rid of all these 84,000 mental afflictions if they're, as you said, 'everywhere'—even if they're not inherently existent?"

Jules' answer was succinct, "By practicing dharma. And through this practice, developing wisdom, diligence, awareness, mindfulness, and vigilance."

Sizing up Jules' answer in his mind, Troy asked, "But, how?"

"By understanding what's at stake, by understanding what's to be gained by striving to eliminate them, and by understanding and putting into practice the methods that will allow you to reduce them." Jules stood from the stool. "You have to bring the contemplation of all of this into your meditation until you see it clearly in your mind. Once you sense that clarity, then you hold that clarity with as much stability in your mind as you can; like a candle flame unmoved by the slightest breeze. This in turn will bring realizations you carry with you into your daily life. That's how meditation practice directly works to bring about very practical results. Think about it, if these practices actually produce realizations and changes in your mind, how could you not bring those changes with you into your daily life?"

Jules stood and walked to the tall set of shelves where he kept customers' instruments waiting to be worked on, and pulled an unstrung guitar from one of the lower shelves. "Since the results of your dharma practice move with you from the meditation cushion into your life, we can bring dharma practice into everything and anything we do. Whatever we've got going on in life, whatever we're in the midst of is a vehicle for waking up if we can be mindful of what's really happening.

"So now, I'm going to help you do some work on this guitar and while you're at it, by harnessing your imagination, you'll begin developing equanimity. You'll also get a taste of reducing your mental afflictions. The most notoriously obstinate and destructive mental affliction of all—the one that is the root obstacle to developing wisdom and compassion, is called self-grasping or ignorance. Are you familiar with that?"

Whoever has self-importance is destroyed by it,
Is disturbed and has no self-confidence.
For those with self-confidence do not succumb to the power of the enemy,
Whereas the former are under the sway of the enemy of self-importance.
VII. 56

Troy recalled the way Mrs. Sternau described self-grasping during one of their visits.

"I think it has something to do with the wrong view or the wrong way we think about something that we consider to be our 'self,' right?" he began. "It's that inherently existing conundrum." He smiled and added, "It's kinda weird how terms like 'inherently existent' have become part of my regular vocabulary!"

"I know what you mean," Jules said. "Different words are required for different conditions! So, what do you understand self-grasping to be?"

"Well," Troy searched his memory of that afternoon, sitting next to Mrs. Sternau, her white hair neatly pinned into a bun. "Mrs. Sternau described self-grasping as being similar to seeing the reflection of the moon in the water and believing that its reflection is the moon itself. If you were to think it's really the moon, you might even try to lift it from the water. But, obviously the moon's not there—the moon depends on the water in order to reflect it like a mirror. I think this must be like what you were saying about the mind being like a mirror too. We see our own existence in that same delusional way—we think we have some kind of permanent self that exists and that we can hold onto in this form as we move through life. But if you really look for it and try to point to where it is, you realize that our mind, body, and all other things we meet in the world and within ourselves are only a collection of parts that are all constantly changing based on how they dependently arise for us, due to our ripening karma. And there's nowhere specifically within all those changing collection of parts that you can point to and say, 'Ah ha! There's a permanent self that never changes!'"

"Well done," Jules said. "So, all of it, ourselves and all other phenomenon are nothing more than dependently arising objects, and therefore there really isn't anything to grasp onto. All things are dependently arisen, like the moon reflected on the water. But, what's the problem with self-grasping? If everyone's got this self-grasping thing going on, why do you suppose we'd want to break from tradition and give it up?"

"Honestly, Jules, I don't know. Why?"

"Because we get hung up on protecting and serving this self, this thing that doesn't really exist, at least not in the way we mistakenly think of it. And because we're hung up on doing that, if we don't work to actively change this fundamental mistaken view, we'll keep seeing and experiencing all things the wrong way, which only leads to more and more self-grasping in all that we do. That—self-grasping—is actually the root mental affliction of ignorance. And from this ignorance is where all hell breaks loose over and over again. You offend me therefore I'll offend you. You take something of mine therefore I'll take something of yours. Your girlfriend smiled at someone else, or you think someone else is paying too much attention to her, and you get jealous. How do all these people we've named 'you' or 'me' in these scenarios really exist? Do you begin to see how ludicrous it all is? Like trying to fight with someone that is only a reflection in a pool of water. There's nothing substantially there!"

"I get it!" Troy interjected. "That's how we screw up over and over again. So, self-grasping actually blocks our ability to have a clear picture of seeing the real nature of all things and how we ourselves and everything we bump into in life actually exists and functions."

"Exactly!" Jules agreed. "Through learning dharma, applying it in meditation practice, and then bringing the results of that practice with us out into the world, we see and experience how things truly are. Through practice, we dissolve our self-grasping which in turn opens the way to reduce and eventually eliminate ignorance and hatred from our mind. Through our practice we also cultivate wisdom and compassion which delivers an experience of inner peace that allows for a more peaceful outer environment as well.

"We must begin in meditation by learning to use a specific practice as an antidote to our mistaken way of seeing all things. It's only then that we can bring that correct view of seeing—the view that has dissolved self-grasping—into our daily life and in everything we do through actions of body, speech, and mind. That's the result of joyous effort in our practice, and the accompanying experience of peace, joy, and happiness."

Troy had observed the relationship between meditation and its influence on things actually changing, including his own actions of self-grasping. The improvement in his relationship with Maureen could never have happened without reflection and actual meditation on the dharma teaching he learned. It made sense that it would be a prerequisite for the transformation that Jules was talking about.

"Okay," Jules said. "Then let's go beyond the space of talking, to actually beginning a very simple practice. You're going to learn to do fret leveling, and while you're at it, you'll apply a specific mindfulness practice on equanimity, turning what you're doing into a meditation practice. In Buddhist practice, we call this 'in between session' practice."

~

If I feel that I never have enough sensual objects
Which are like honey smeared upon a razor's edge,
Then why should I ever feel that I have enough
Merit which ripens in happiness and peace?
VII. 65

Troy followed Jules over to the workbench in the center of the room and watched as Jules supported the guitar's neck in a padded vise and rested the body of the guitar on a patch of carpeting attached to the workbench.

"Okay, so fret leveling is a routine job that requires patience and a lot of focus—qualities we learn and acquire in actual analytical meditation." He pulled a file from the pegboard where most of his tools hung on the wall behind him. "This guitar has a lot of buzzes. The problem is, the frets are worn and the tops of the frets are flat and scratchy with little dents that come from the strings being pressed against them over time. To eliminate the buzzes and improve the overall sound, all the frets need to be made level with each other and then crowned so there's a single point of contact with the string. So, I've already taken the strings off and now we've got to gradually bring the high spots level with the others." He held the file and began to demonstrate the technique for Troy as he explained, "We need to file across the top of the frets; following the curvature of the radius of the neck, they should all be level with no highs or lows in relation to each other." Troy watched, studying how Jules manipulated the file and noticing the steadiness of each motion.

"So, the meditation part is this," Jules continued. "We can reflect on our own tendency to view some people as being close to us—you know, like the favorite people in our lives—while there are others that we feel hatred toward or who are just generally annoying and so we really wish they'd just go away. Then there are a lot of people that don't even register on our radar; we barely give them a thought one way or the other. While you're leveling off the highs and lows on the frets, contemplate the benefits of viewing all beings with equanimity. Just as the unevenness of frets creates disturbances in the quality of the guitar's sound, so our own lack of equanimity creates disturbances in the way we resonate or dependently arise with the world around us." Jules eyed the work he'd begun and then handed the file to Troy and helped him position it in his hand for the best angle. "Okay, so look at the frets in relation with each other; there can be high spots, see? Now try to bring them gradually even with the others so they'll all work together." After he had seen that Troy was getting the knack of using the file, he told him to bring to mind the people closest to him, those he loved most and to imagine extending that same feeling to everyone equally, even to the people who are the thorns in his side; leveling the frets while leveling the jagged edges of his own biases. Jules left him to do this while he returned to add polish to the fret board of another guitar, sweetening the air with the scent of beeswax and lemon oil.

The two worked in silence filled only by the steady whir of the ceiling fan, the soft rhythmic grating from the file moving over the frets, Jules' polishing cloth sliding against the wood, and the intermittent songs of warblers and cardinals reporting on the day's events.

After a while Jules came to check Troy's progress, pointing out a few places he'd missed. Once everything was level he took another file from the pegboard, "This is a triangle file and we're going to use this to do the crowning, that's where we round off all the edges in order to leave each fret with a high 'crown' along its top." He pulled a red marker from his shirt pocket, uncapped it and drew a line along the center top of each fret. "I'll show you how to carefully sort of roll this file so you don't let any portion of the line disappear while you form the perfect shape." He then demonstrated how Troy should angle his hand at about 45° and gently roll while drawing the file to work on the sides of the frets until each is smooth and rounded. "The result becomes that single point of contact between the fret and string that I mentioned before. Like the single point in meditation between yourself and the object of your meditation." Troy took the file and tried to duplicate Jules' motions. They passed the file back and forth between them as Jules helped Troy refine the technique. "That's it," he said. "You've got it now." He kept a close watch on the file, pointing out the smooth, burnished edges between each of the three sides to help prevent scarring the fret board itself. "Okay, so your meditation while you're doing the crowning is to imagine that you're also filing away, or reducing, your mental afflictions. Self-grasping, anger, hatred, pride, jealousy, greed, covetousness, resentment, attachment to all the many things that truly have no ability to deliver any form of lasting happiness and that show up in obsessive thoughts like craving and desire. The list goes on of course, but you get the idea. Then, imagine the peace, the absolute freedom that follows when all those afflictions are finally gone."

Troy laughed and said, "Okay, I'll try to keep all of that in mind." He set to work, focusing initially on carefully rolling the file the way Jules had shown him and smoothing the edges until he had absorbed the rhythm and motion of the process and his technique became more fluid. Then he applied the meditative aspect Jules had instructed him to engage in, filing away his own self-grasping—the root mental affliction that permeates all the others. He thought about his own attachment to himself, all the things he thought of as "mine" like possessions, friends, even Maggie and how anything or anyone that threatened anything he had labeled as belonging to him would bring out anger, hatred or jealousy. He thought about pride, and the many times he'd been unwilling to receive advice and instead was reactive as if even well-intended suggestions had been veiled criticism. Nothing other than self-grasping would produce these reactive responses. Self-grasping was there, even if seemingly quiet for the moment, like a coiled snake poised to strike. As he analyzed each of these mental afflictions, he checked again to see if any of them had a fixed and permanent nature of their own. The answer was "no." The process was similar to taking a puzzle apart until no picture remains. He used the image of puzzle pieces to see his own self-grasping as nothing more than pieces he himself had assembled. He then expanded the metaphor to view this disassembled state, or the innumerable causes and conditions, as being the actual truth of how all things exist. He held his mind singularly focused in this awareness and experienced the sense of self-grasping dissolve. There was nothing to hold or grasp onto. And therefore, absolutely everything became possible.

The crowning process took longer than the initial leveling and even within all the motions of filing there was stillness; the calm stillness that comes when the mind is focused, like the mirror surface of a lake that obscures the hidden activity of the life it nourishes. Jules was restringing the guitar he had just finished polishing, and peered over the top of his glasses to watch Troy's progress, observing his technique, and so much more. The shadows outside lengthened, and the light that came through the windows dimmed. With the last string wound, Jules began tuning the instrument, breaking the silence with the sound of each string dipping and rising, tightening, loosening and tightening again into the right pitch. He strummed a few chords, played a couple of riffs, assessed its tone and then returned the guitar to the shelf. He scribbled some notes into the notebook he kept on a string attached to the bottom shelf and then walked back to where Troy was crowning the last couple of frets at the low end of the fret board.

"Nicely done, Troy. The more you do this, the more you'll master the technique. This, by the way, is true of meditation too."

Jules presented Troy with another tool. "This is a dressing stick. See the little piece of sand paper here?" He pointed to the underside of the wooden stick that was about the size of a thick pencil. "We'll use this to polish off the little bits of scratch on the frets." Troy watched again while Jules polished the first few frets. "While you're doing this you can rejoice in the positive force of karmic potential that comes as a result of the meditation you just did. 'Rejoice' is a great word if you think about it; you're celebrating something that has significant value. Think of the virtue; the positive momentum you are building and understand that it is actually strengthening you as you develop your capacity to benefit all other beings. And if you think about the karmic potential of rejoicing, you can really appreciate how it gives a boost to and strengthens all that potential you've just generated through your practice."

"Okay, that makes sense," Troy said, noticing the sensation of building momentum resulting from his previous effort.

Jules handed the dressing stick to Troy. "Great. Here you go then; get to it!"

Troy began polishing the frets and reflected on the meditation that Jules had given him. As he did this, he felt an actual sensation as if there were a lightening, or something like an opening into more spaciousness… or maybe, he thought, it was a sense of true freedom. He found it hard to pin a word on it, but it came along with a conviction that "liberation" is not just a term thrown around in philosophical discussions, but is a state of mind that is possible to achieve. He recalled what Jules had just told him. *Yes*, he thought, *this is definitely something to rejoice in. And, it actually makes perfect sense to dedicate my effort on this path for the benefit of all beings.*

He ran his fingers over each of the frets, bent down a little more closely to examine them from a different angle and then, satisfied, he looked at Jules and said, "I think it's done."

Jules nodded, and with a slight smile, "Yeah, I think you're right." He loosened the clasp of the vise and lifted the guitar, "Nicely done, Troy." He stood, holding the guitar and then with an afterthought set it back down on the table.

Next to the pegboard were rows of small bins, each labeled with its contents. He reached into one of the bins and pulled out a package of strings and tossed them onto the table next to Troy.

"So, here's a guitar, right?" he said. "It has no strings, we can't play it, but we still call it a guitar. And now here's a set of strings. So, where's the true guitar? Is it in the strings? Is it in the curved pieces of wood? Or is it in the thin flat pieces? Is it in the fret board? Or that hole, or maybe even this bridge? How about the tuning pegs? Maybe it's in the empty space inside the guitar? Where is the 'self' of the guitar?"

Troy laughed, "Um, you've got me, Jules. When you put it like that I honestly don't know."

"Okay, then," Jules said, casting a glance at the clock on the wall. "Do you have more time or do you need to be on your way?"

"I've got time," Troy said.

"Great, let's get this guitar ready to be strung." He brought it over to the table where he'd been working before. He used a soft brush to sweep away any loose filings that remained and then poured polish from a bottle of beeswax and lemon oil onto a piece of cloth. "I just use small circular motions to polish between each fret; this adds moisture to the fret board and gives it a nice, rich glow." He polished between the top couple of frets and then handed the cloth to Troy. "Here you go." While Troy polished, Jules opened the package of strings.

"What about the rest of the guitar? Do you want me to polish the whole thing?" Troy asked.

"No. You definitely don't want to use lemon oil and beeswax on the rest of the guitar. There are different polishes we use for the body; I'll take care of that tomorrow. I've got a couple of things I want to check out first. But for now, let's just get some strings on it."

Once Troy had strung and tuned the guitar Jules tested it out. "Ah, the buzzes are gone!" Jules closed his eyes to listen closely as he plucked each string and then played a variety of chords, voicing them differently in order to hear the interactions between each of the strings.

"We're going to talk about that thing called 'dependent arising' that we touched on last time you were here. We say that things lack inherent existence because everything arises dependently, in dependence upon causes and conditions. Earlier you and I were exploring and examining to find just where is this thing we call 'self' that we're so stuck on claiming as 'me' and makes us think of all the things we consider to be ours as 'mine.' In other words, 'self-grasping.' And because of self-grasping, we suffer from all that comes with it, that root affliction of ignorance and all its little tendrils and off-shoots like pride, jealousy, greed, and anger. There is no inherently existent, unchanging self that exists someplace in the body or the mind or in consciousness. This thing we think of as our 'self' is perpetually in a state of change. It's not located anywhere we can identify. Yet, we can't say that it exists separately from our body either. In other words, there is a dependently existing 'self,' not an inherently existing one. The 'self' is nothing more than a label, a mere appearance in each moment that we connect to our body and mind."

None of this was entirely new to Troy, but the topic is slippery enough when trying to understand it that he strained to listen intently. He was curious to see where Jules was taking the discussion with the guitar.

"So, we can say that this collection of parts—pieces of wood with different shapes and thicknesses, different types of wood, and coiled pieces of wound and plain steel that we call strings; the empty spaces that allow for a certain vibration of sound to occur, the material that the tuning pegs are made of—all together these parts form something that functions as a guitar. However, the guitar lacks inherent existence because it arose in dependence upon many parts, causes, and conditions. We can take those causes and conditions even further. Before there was wood for the guitar, there had to have been a variety of trees, and before there were trees, there were seeds, soil, sunlight, rain—all the right conditions that happened to all be in the right location for the seed to sprout and grow successfully into a tree. We could even trace those conditions back further and further. Before the soil was rich with nutrients, there were minerals and other decomposing elements, before there was rain, there were clouds, and before there were clouds, there were oceans and lakes, and rivers, and before there were oceans, lakes, and rivers, there was rain. You get the idea. Is there ever a true single element that we can call the essence or inherently existent element that is the unchanging thing we've labeled 'guitar'? No, it isn't anything more than the label we've given it, based on all of its parts arising in dependence upon causes and conditions, most especially the mind that conceived the potential of an instrument in the first place! And then the mind that labeled or named it, 'guitar.' This is true of everything in existence.

"You can apply this analytical meditation to all objects and you'll find the same thing—that there is no inherently existing fixed, unchanging essence. In fact, this is one of the most important meditations you need to spend time engaging in. It's a way to pull back the curtain and see what's really going on. And once you can accomplish that, you'll reveal an entirely new dimension to how you interact with life—compassionately and with a sense of joy and freedom. It is truly the key to the transformation of suffering into happiness."

Jules' words were a lot to absorb. There comes a point of oversaturation, and Troy felt he had reached the tipping point. "So, I get the analytical thing you're driving at. But what do I do with it?"

The answer wasn't quick to come. Jules lowered his head, standing with both hands pressed against the surface of the table.

"What you do with this, Troy, is to recognize that dependent arising is the nature of everything. Absolutely everything. Recognize that dependent arising is active in your feelings, your body, your joys, challenges, relationships, successes, and defeats—in all that you experience. Recognize the role of karma and be mindful of the quality of your intentions through your actions of body, speech, and mind, because through them you are creating your karma. You fill all your intentions and actions with the quality of either virtue or non-virtue. And in doing so, you create the future conditions to dependently arise with a similar quality. I know it probably seems that I'm repeating myself, but I just want to be sure that you have a deep understanding of the fact that nothing truly exists the way it appears, and therefore there is nothing truly substantial to grasp at or to be repelled by. He lifted the guitar from the table and brought it back to the shelf where it would wait for the next day's work. "And I'll also say this again because it is just that important: meditate on this analytically and once you can hold a clear understanding and experience of this, rest in single-pointed focus on dependent-arising nature. It's a very blissful experience. You can then take this experience with you throughout your day and bring it to mind in all your activities of body, speech, and mind. As you deepen your understanding, the roots of wisdom also deepen, and your natural impulse to let go of self-grasping and transform it into caring for others in all that you do will become stronger. With roots of wisdom, no matter what's going on around you, compassion will be your response instead of impatience, discouragement or frustration. These meditations on developing equanimity, eliminating mental afflictions, recognizing dependent arising, and other meditations that you are learning will create the causes and conditions for those two wings of wisdom and compassion to naturally arise in you. Those two wings will carry you safely anywhere."

Therefore, I should aspire for virtue,
And with great respect acquaint myself with it.
Having undertaken the wholesome in the manner of Vajradhvaja[6]
I should then proceed to acquaint myself with self-confidence.
VII. 46

When Troy left Jules' studio, a text was waiting from Maggie. "I'm painting at Mrs. Sternau's. She'd love to see you. If it's not too late when you get back maybe you can cut those branches for her. Let me know when you're on your way, okay? Love you!"

It was already a little past six when he called. "Hey, Mags, I'm just leaving now. Are you still at Mrs. Sternau's?"

"Yeah, I'm just cleaning up. Can you stop by?"

"Sure, I should be there in about half an hour. Is that soon enough?"

---

6 *Avatamsaka Sutra, Thog. P. 144,* 'For example, Devaputra, when the sun shines forth it illuminates any suitable place without being turned back by such obstacles as blindness in people or uneven mountain formations. Likewise when a Bodhisattva shines forth for the sake of others he ripens and liberates any suitable disciple and is not turned back by the various obstacles present in sentient beings.'

"I'm sure that's fine. I'll leave the easel set up so you can see the painting I'm working on. I'll let Mrs. Sternau know you're on your way. Truthfully, I think cutting the branches is just an excuse so she can see you."

"Well, I want to see her too," Troy said.

"Yeah, well, if she were about seventy years younger, I'd be getting jealous about now," Maggie laughed.

On the heels of the dharma he and Jules had just been discussing, Troy couldn't help but notice that even in a light-hearted moment, self-grasping is so universally and readily accepted as normal that jealousy over a shared warmth between two people, if one of the two has been labeled as "mine," is easily understood as a threat to that fabrication of a self.

"I can tell you with no doubt whatsoever," Troy reassured her, "there will never be a true reason for you to feel jealous."

~

Just like those who yearn for the fruits of play,
(Bodhisattvas) are attracted
To whatever task they may do:
They never have enough, it only brings them joy.
VII. 63

It was a different assortment of flowers in bloom since the last time Troy had been to Mrs. Sternau's house. The season's turnings had brought clusters of hydrangeas spilling white flowers like marble fountains, creamy-pink dahlias, and cosmos. As he approached the front door, he saw Mrs. Sternau's silhouette through the dark screen.

"Hello, darling, please come in," she greeted him, pushing the door open for him while she steadied herself against her cane.

She appeared thinner and frailer than when he saw her last, yet her voice was as clear and strong, and her eyes every bit as penetrating when she asked, "How have you been, dear?"

"I'm doing pretty well, thanks," he said. "How about you?"

"I have nothing to complain about," she said. "Especially on a day like this that's just about as beautiful as days come. And, I've had the pleasure of having your lovely Maggie here to paint. I believe she might be transforming Albert's garden into a scene from an Impressionist's dream." She took Troy's arm for support, "Come. Let's see what she has painted."

They walked together slowly, arm in arm, over the gravel pathway that wound through the garden to where Maggie was putting her brushes and paints back into her paint-stained canvas bag.

"Well, now my picture's complete!" Maggie said when she saw Troy. "Hey, hon," she said softly as Troy leaned to kiss her. "It's still a work in progress," she said gesturing to the painting that was resting on the easel. "I have fallen in love with these Japanese Anemones. There's something so graceful about the way they soften the edges of the rocks that's just so beautiful." She had filled the entire canvas with long, intertwining stems lined with unopened buds as well as those that were opened into delicate white-pink flowers. She painted each flower with its colony of tiny, yellow-knobbed stamen centers, some having caught the spilled dustings of yellow that had fallen onto the petals themselves like wet gold in a miner's pan. Maggie had revealed just enough of the garden's rock-lined border in the lower portion of the canvas to contrast the delicate lines of the flowers with granite flecked by sunlight on quartz; the low light illuminating even the undersides of the paper-thin petals. In essence, light was everywhere, even within the specks of dark soil that was almost unnoticeable and could easily have been overlooked had it not been for the fact that Troy had learned from Maggie to overlook nothing when you see the world through an artist's eyes.

Mrs. Sternau's strength was noticeably less than even just a few weeks earlier, and the weight of her hand pulled a little more heavily against Troy's arm. Troy suggested she take a seat on the white bench a few yards away under the shade of the beech trees. Their pace was slow with evenly measured steps across the lawn until they reached the bench. Troy kept his hand on her arm to steady her as she lowered herself to sit. "Ah, this feels delightful. Thank you." She rested while Troy helped Maggie gather her supplies.

"I think you're getting it, Mags," Troy said.

"Getting what?"

"You said you wanted to capture the light and the peace of this place."

"You think so?" she asked. "I think it needs something more." She stood back from the painting, her arms folded, watching the canvas as if within it she could see movement. "I'll sleep on it. Something'll come to me."

"Speaking of sleep," Troy said quietly, nodding to where Mrs. Sternau sat dozing under the beech trees, her head tipped gently forward.

"Oh no, what'll we do?" Maggie whispered. "I don't want to wake her up, but we can't just leave her out here."

"We can hang here for a while." Troy said, his eyes on Mrs. Sternau. "I'll take your easel up to the porch. Our beach towels are still in the truck, I'll go grab one for us to sit on."

Troy returned with a towel tucked loosely under his arm. As he spread it out on the grass the briny scent from the beach released like a memory set free. He and Maggie sat together, talking softly about this and that while Maggie ran her fingers through the grass searching for four leaf clovers. Eventually, the sun dropped lazily to the place on the horizon where it turned the sky shades of watermelon and peach. A pair of squirrels chased each other up the shagbark hickory tree and leaped from branch to branch, chattering noisily in pursuit of something only they understood.

A cool breeze woke Mrs. Sternau from her nap. "Oh, I'm so sorry, I dozed off again. I've been doing that all day. But I'm delighted to open my eyes to see you here." She turned toward the sunset, taking it in as if she were drinking its colors. "Do you feel the hints of September announcing itself?" she asked, savoring the air as she drew a slow breath. "You can feel it in the breezes, and if you pay attention, you'll find it in the scent of soil blending with ripening apples and grapes." She turned her face toward the dusk-lit sky and said, "Soon the light will begin to shift from this soft, intoxicating summer light to the sharper, crisp autumn light that brings focus to things to come."

Troy alerted his senses, not only to see, feel, and smell what Mrs. Sternau described, but also to understand what might be the fuller meaning of what she had said.

"This is life. All its perceived comings and goings do not truly arise nor do they truly perish. It is life's dance of infinite particles in a constant state of change." She laughed, "It's all truly quite joyful."

Troy enjoyed the poetic way she described the essence of what Jules had just been describing as dependent arising.

Maggie stopped sorting through the blades of grass and stems of clover, and raised her face toward the sky. With eyes closed, she breathed the air to see if she could smell the scents Mrs. Sternau described. "I can't smell anything. Can you, Troy?"

"Nope. Not really."

"It's there," Mrs. Sternau said. "Stay aware. You'll find it another day."

"Speaking of changing light, Mrs. Sternau, while we still have some, where are the branches you'd like me to cut?" Troy asked.

"To the left of the porch," she pointed above the terrace, "you'll see two branches that are obstructing the light by the living room window. Neither is terribly thick. You won't need a ladder if you use Albert's old pole saw. It's in the crawl space where we found the vase for your stepmother's garden."

"Okay, I'll go take care of it."

"Maggie, darling, let's go inside before the mosquitos discover us. I hope you and Troy will stay for supper. I have tomato soup and fresh cucumbers for cucumber sandwiches."

"Sounds delicious," Maggie said, taking her arm as they walked together up the steps to the terrace and through the porch into the house.

~

So, having mounted the horse of an Awakening Mind
That dispels all discouragement and weariness,
Who when they know of this mind that proceeds
from joy to joy
Would ever lapse into despondency?
VII. 30

After dinner, Maggie stepped out of the room to get something from her purse. Mrs. Sternau leaned across the table and reached for Troy's hand. She lowered her voice to just above a whisper, "Whatever comes, know that its wisdom will be revealed only through your practice. Therefore, you must not waste time, and you must take care not to miss an opportunity to practice. And darling, when you're truly awake, every moment is an opportunity to practice." At that, Maggie came back into the room, and Mrs. Sternau picked up the conversation they were having previously about the movie she had recently watched with her granddaughter, *Midnight in Paris*.

"Have you seen that film?" she asked.

"Yes, we loved it," Maggie said. "Paris in the 1920s must've been fabulous. I would've loved to have been there then."

"I'm sure it was," Mrs. Sternau agreed. "My granddaughter wanted to know if I could go back in time, to what time would I return." She laughed and said, "I told her I can visit any time in my mind any time I choose and that's good enough for me."

With that comment, Troy wondered if time, too, was empty of inherent existence, but tucked that thought away to think about later along with the advice Mrs. Sternau had just given him.

"I would've hung out with the musicians," he said. "I'm not a jazz player now, but I think I would've been one then."

"It's fun to speculate on what might have been," Mrs. Sternau said. "But it can be much more joyful and beneficial to contemplate the potential you wish to develop in the future and then take active measures toward that goal."

"Well, I'm inspired by those artists of the past," Maggie said. "Their work inspires me to develop my own potential as an artist."

"Indeed, there is value in observing and learning from the masters of the past." Mrs. Sternau shot a glance at Troy and added, "Even the masters had to begin with the fundamentals at some point, so if you keep that in mind it can encourage you to be patient as you do the same."

~

Rita was folding a basket of laundry, piling clothes and towels neatly folded on the couch when Troy got home. She paused the movie she'd been watching; the actors' faces frozen mid-sentence and mid-expression on the screen.

"Hi honey," she said. "I was hoping you'd be getting home soon."

"Well, I'm here. What's up?"

"I'm heading down to Michelle's tomorrow morning to visit Uncle Jonathan. Michelle said he still hasn't gotten his strength back, so we both thought a visit might lift his spirits."

"Do you want me to go with you?"

"That's okay," she said. "I'll be staying with Michelle—we'll help each other."

Although he would have gone in a heartbeat, with only a couple of weeks until classes were scheduled to begin, he was relieved to stay home. He was inspired to continue the practice Jules had given him, spend time reading, and wanted to have more meetings with Jules. If all went well, he would be graduating in the spring and then a different kind of work would begin. Troy had decisions to make in order to be ready for that time when he would need to determine what kind of work to pursue. One thing he already knew was that whatever choice he made would be informed by his dharma practice. He felt that his dharma practice was similar to keeping his guitar in tune. Out of tune, it didn't matter how good his technique was, the guitar's sound would be bad, and without his dharma practice, his life would be lived out of tune.

"Okay, Mom. I'll take care of the house while you're away." He laughed and added, "Don't worry—I won't throw any parties while you're gone!"

"Thank God I don't have to worry about things like that anymore," she said, tossing the towel she had just folded onto the pile on the couch. "Look at these grey hairs I've got—you and your brothers can claim ownership of at least a few."

"Sorry, Mom."

"That's okay," she said. "You know I wouldn't trade being your mom for anything in the world. Besides, the divorce contributed its share too, and that had nothing to do with you guys."

"Yeah, those were some pretty dark days for all of us," Troy said. Then, changing the subject to something less weighty, "What time are you leaving in the morning?"

"Most likely around eight-thirty."

"I'm working breakfast tomorrow, so I'll be leaving before you, but I'll see you in the morning. You'll be up early, won't you?"

"Oh yeah, I'll definitely be up early." Rita looked at him through a frown of concern, one that had creased so frequently over the years that her face had adopted it as a permanent feature. "You're going to bed already? Are you feeling okay?"

"Yeah, Mom, I'm fine," he said. It felt awkward to say more, to say that he was going to sit on a cushion and meditate for a while. Ever since he'd left Jules' he was eager to revisit the meditations and contemplation Jules had introduced him to as well as to consider the words Mrs. Sternau had whispered over supper. Would his mother understand his commitment to something like meditation? Or might she be offended, or find it weird? And then decisively and with no apology or elaboration he said, "Um, I'm just gonna go meditate for a bit, okay?"

"Oh?" The frown line changed to a single raised eyebrow that, without saying a single word, conveyed that she found something to be humorously off. "Okay, then. Good night, honey," and she teasingly lowered her voice about an octave, "Ooooommmmm."

~

"Likewise in all these situations
I shall acquaint myself with mindfulness."
With this (motivation) as a cause, I shall aspire
To meet (with teachers) or accomplish the tasks (they assign me).
VII.74

As he settled himself onto the cushion, he brought his mind's focus to his breath as if his mind were a passenger on his breath—entering, leaving, and entering his body again and again. He noticed that his level of distraction at night was distinctly greater than early in the morning and found quieting his mind to be especially difficult. *Every moment is an opportunity to practice,* Mrs. Sternau had said. If that is true, how could he turn a distracted mind into being part of his practice? Jules had said that the quality of the mind is emptiness and therefore it has the capacity to change. Maybe distraction is just an uncontrolled aspect of that changeability, which means it can change from being distracted to being focused. In other words, like everything else, if the mind is impermanent then of course distraction is too. Instead of fighting it, he allowed his distraction to dissolve into focus, and brought his mind's attention back again to his breath.

Cultivating the ability to maintain focus was crucial in order to nurture the strength of his practice. By training his mind to develop focus and awareness of the object of his meditation, he could begin to reduce his mental afflictions and eventually end the negative karma that follows in their footsteps. With awareness he could also gain merit and virtue, the fuel or positive potential that clears obstructions to the path. For Troy, this path was not about religion. It was a path of peace and a path of happiness. Troy didn't view all the many buddhas Jules had mentioned as representatives of a religion or as celestial beings that hover over and favor a particular, devoted group of people. He saw them as beings that exist as a continuum of compassion and love, as the embodiment of energy focused purely for the benefit of all sentient beings.

It was that first meeting with Grace when Troy discovered the dharma that allowed him to experience his potential for being compassionate. With this essential connection, he began little by little to shed his own pain and ignorance while he focused his effort to develop wisdom and compassion. Maureen had been the perfect person to apply this effort toward by recognizing her aggressive behaviors were in fact symptoms of her own very deep suffering, and that his own negative responses to her during their interaction, only perpetuated both their pain. With this understanding he could see that his own peace ultimately depended on her peace. Then, the opportunity to respond to her with compassion rather than a force of anger and hostility to match hers was not only doable, it felt like the only effective path of action to take, resulting in the transformation of their interactions into something much more positive.

He brought his mind to the fret leveling meditation he had done earlier with Jules, a leveling of all his biases of attachment and aversion. He sat on his cushion, deepening that meditation by using self-grasping as his focus. His mind opened into a vast space where the ordinary agitations and inner chatter quieted into a state of calm and where a quiet, gentle presence unfolded in his heart like a flower opening under the warmth of the August sun. His concentration now steady and focused naturally flowed into single-pointed stillness. Troy felt this experience was another confirmation that transformation is possible, and that impermanence is a beautiful thing when mindful intention is brought into focus.

If I find myself amidst a crowd of disturbing conceptions,
I shall endure them in a thousand ways;
Like a lion among foxes,
I will not be affected by this disturbing host.
VII. 60

It was that time of day when the moon begins to show itself as a pale white globe in the blue of the sky and the sun makes its descent, the two positioned momentarily like a balanced see-saw, neither higher than the other. The scent of pine and earth was ripe with life, and the woods swarmed with sounds—locusts, the occasional mosquito, cardinals' songs, and the hollow percussive tones from a woodpecker drilling into a distant tree. As Troy and Maggie made their way along the trail bordered by gnarly branches of sweet-smelling mountain laurel, and past chipmunks that swished through dry fallen leaves, Troy realized that for anyone to think they could truly be alone in these woods was clearly mistaken.

A steep climb brought them to a view that overlooked a stretch of ridges and lakes. Catching their breath, they stood together on the rock ledge where golden-green patches of moss spread like tapestry, and where pine infused breezes spiraled from nowhere and everywhere. The silence was pristine. They stood quietly together, watching the light move on the water that creased against itself under breezes that slid across the lake. Air puffed under the fabric of Troy's shirt, cooling the perspiration that had formed on his skin; his body felt porous—as if it breathed indivisibly with all of existence.

"We should do this more often," Maggie said, reaching for Troy's hand. "If the world stopped turning right at this moment, I'd be content to take all this, holding your hand into eternity!"

"Be careful what you wish for, Mags! It's not that I wouldn't want to always be close to you, but even this moment would get old after a while."

"Troy, why do you always have to be so damn serious about everything?" Maggie pulled her hand from his and gave him a knock on his arm. "Okay, so there goes that moment of perfection. Let's keep walking."

They walked down the other side of the hill, stepping sideways, carefully navigating the steeper slopes, rocks sliding under their feet until they reached a small stream someone had stretched a log across to form a makeshift bridge. They crossed the stream and followed its course, kicking their way through leaves, and twigs that cracked beneath their feet.

Troy began to worry; had he in fact grown too serious from all this reflection and dharma study he had been doing? Had he lost his ability to just let things be and enjoy a simple conversation for what it was without analyzing every statement? The practice was supposed to be about joy, he thought. Had he lost the point?

And on the heels of that thought, his phone rang; a deer sprang from the cluster of white pines and disappeared from sight at the edge of a hill.

"Hi, Mom, what's up?"

"It's Uncle Jonathan," she said. "It's time. You need to come now if you can."

~

If someone dropped a sword during a battle,
They would immediately pick it up out of fear.
Likewise, if I lose the weapon of mindfulness,
I should quickly retrieve it, being afraid of hell.
VII. 69

Mrs. Sternau's words echoed quietly again in Troy's mind while he waited for Jules to answer the phone, *Whatever comes, know that its wisdom will be revealed only through your practice...when you're truly awake, every moment is an opportunity to practice.*

"Hello?"

"Jules, hey; it's Troy."

"Hi. What's up?"

"My uncle's not doing well. Um, he's not gonna make it, and my mother wants me to get there soon as possible. So, I'm sorry but I'm not going to be able to be there on Wednesday."

"Oh, I'm sorry to hear that. About your uncle, I mean. Are you okay?"

"I guess, yeah, I'm fine," he paused. "Well, maybe not totally fine." Troy paced slowly on the small porch outside his bedroom, sweeping fallen pine needles from the railing with his hand. "What do I do? I mean, how do I help? What do you say to someone who's getting ready to leave this life?"

Troy heard Jules drag a chair along the floor, and pictured him sitting by one of the open windows in his studio. "Well, generally, I think that as someone is nearing death the best thing we can offer is to be a calming, reassuring presence. It's not necessary to say a lot. Find ways to acknowledge all the good he's done in life; it'll help him to hold his mind in a positive place. The quality of mind at the time of death has a very powerful effect on what follows. Even if he's not talking, he can hear your words. You've known him since you were a kid, so coming up with things to thank him for or to acknowledge him for won't be difficult. You can encourage your mother to do the same. Honor his faith if he has one—don't confuse him by talking about the dharma or things he's not familiar with. Very simply, just help him to be comfortable, peaceful and to know he is loved and that his life has been meaningfully lived."

Tears welled in Troy's eyes. "That helps, Jules. Thank you."

"Oh, and Troy, one more thing."

"Okay?"

"What I just told you is for your uncle's benefit. Now, this is for yours. Use this as an opportunity to meditate on dependent arising and to contemplate life's impermanence. Seriously. It's important. The impermanence of this life is something that won't change. Death will come to each of us no matter what. This is true for your uncle, for all living beings and of course for you and me too. Even though you are young and it seems a long way off, you must prepare for your own death. So, as you think about dependent arising, understand that death and birth is also a dependent arising. As the Dalai Lama says, death is like simply stepping out of one set of clothes and into new ones.

"There is a verse from *The Foundation of All Good Qualities* that says:

This life is as impermanent as a water bubble
Remember how quickly it decays and death comes.
After death, just like a shadow follows the body
The results of black and white karma follow.[7]

"So, it is truly essential to live your life with the awareness of its definite impermanence. And when you do live this way, you won't waste the opportunity this human life provides you with to cultivate all the ingredients of merit and wisdom, those two wings we've talked about that will carry you forward in this life and beyond—in other words, your next set of clothes. You can imagine that through your actions you are actually weaving the fabric for your next garment now. Right

---

7 Lama Tsongkhapa's famous prayer, *The Foundation of All Good Qualities*, is the most concise and stirring outline available of the Lam-Rim teachings. In only fourteen stanzas, Tsongkhapa offers us a prayer that covers the entire graduated path to enlightenment, short enough to recite every day, profound enough to study for a lifetime. https://fpmt.org/mandala/archives/mandala-issues-for-2007/august/the-foundation-of-all-good-qualities/

now, you're in the prime of your physical strength and health, so you're probably pretty content with your present body. But speaking from personal experience, although the body's decline is gradual there comes a point when you actually look forward to trading this body in. This is my long-winded way of saying, let joy be the shoes you wear on this path as you live a life dedicated to benefitting all, and cultivating merit and wisdom. If you do, as you move forward in this life and most important, at the time of death you will be free of regrets."

"This is good, Jules. Thank you," Troy said, shooing a mosquito away and leaving the porch to go back inside. "I guess I better get packed and hit the road. It'll be late by the time I get there. Hopefully I'll make it in time."

"You can only do your best; beyond that, things are out of your control."

~

It was nearly two o'clock in the morning when Troy arrived at hospice. He stood outside his truck; the clicking engine was percussion in the dark stillness. He inhaled the damp August night and arched his back to stretch, seeing where clouds had arranged themselves like grey chiffon flower petals around the moon.

It was time. He drew in a long breath, imagining he could gather strength and wisdom from the night's humid embrace, and walked toward the lamplight of the entryway.

He approached the reception area at the end of the dimly lit corridor. A woman working at the desk slid the window open, "May I help you?" she asked.

"Yes, I'm here to see Jonathan Skalzoni."

"Your name please?"

"Troy Riley."

"Please sign in here," she gestured to the clipboard on the counter. "I'll have someone show you to his room. It'll be just a moment."

Troy added his name to the list, several names below where he noticed that his mother and Michelle hadn't yet signed out. He was relieved they were still there; maybe he wasn't too late.

An older woman came from the office behind the reception area, her stride undeterred by a slight limp. "You're here to see Mr. Skalzoni?"

"Yes," he said. "How is he?"

"Well, we are keeping him comfortable by keeping his mouth moist and giving him medications to relieve any discomfort he may be experiencing," she explained as they walked slowly toward Jonathan's room. "His brain and his kidneys have shut down, so he won't be able to speak to you, but he can hear. Even in this state, people are aware of what's going on around them and can hear conversations and words spoken to them. So, we encourage you to share your kind and heartfelt thoughts with him. And because they're also very sensitive to touch, soft, gentle physical contact is best."

How does she even know what he's aware of or what he can hear? Troy wondered. Her voice sounded distant but oddly confident. Troy pulled his mind back from the weight of his own grief to the guidance Jules had prepared him with. To benefit Jonathan, Troy wouldn't burden him with his own sadness.

The woman gently placed her hand against Troy's arm and said, "Being with someone as they transition from this life can be a profound experience. Whether we're with someone at the time of birth or their time of death, we witness something that is packed with mystery and love." She lowered her voice just above a whisper, "Okay, here's his room. Do you have any questions before we go in?"

"No. Thank you," he said. "I'm ready."

~

At such a time when my mind is developed
To the point of regarding my body like food,
Then what hardship would there be
When it came to giving away my flesh?
VII. 26

In the soft light that filtered from the hallway into his room, Jonathan seemed to be sleeping comfortably. Rita and Michelle were sleeping as well, each curled up on small sofas. *Appearances can be deceiving*, Troy thought. Although they all looked as if they were doing the same thing, Jonathan was doing something quite different. He was actively in the process of dying. His organs were shutting down. This was the last time Troy would see him alive. Every muscle in Troy's body tightened around his heart and throat into a wall of grief. Jonathan had been a rock for Troy's family, a bigger-than-life presence who always conveyed reassurance that somehow, no matter what was going on, everything would be okay.

Rita sat up when she heard Troy come in the room. Their eyes met; there were no words. She stood to embrace him. Their tears fell in silence except for the sound of breath moist with sorrow. It wasn't clear whose grief he felt more, his mother's or his own, but it hurt with knee-jarring force. Michelle awoke and stood, slowly straightening as if pulled by a marionette's string. Again, there were no words, just another tearful embrace.

"Would you like some time alone with him?" Michelle asked.

Troy nodded and whispered, "Yeah, thanks."

He stood by Jonathan's bedside and placed his hand gently on Jonathan's while he waited for his mother and Michelle to leave. Jonathan's hand was cold, and his skin was mottled purplish. "I'm here Uncle Jonathan," he paused, breathing space into the sadness that clenched his throat. "It's me, Troy." Jonathan's hand twitched beneath Troy's. He watched Jonathan's face for some indication of recognition but there was no movement whatsoever. "You've been so good to my mom, my brothers and to me over all these years. Thank you for all the little ways—and the big ways—you've helped us and made our lives happier." It was odd to speak with someone who was incapable of replying. It reminded Troy of scenes in movies when someone goes with a heavy heart for confession. The priest, behind a drape listens in silence while the confessor pours out his heart. But at some point, the priest offers instruction about how to go forward, and how to make amends. None of that would be coming from Jonathan.

"Do you remember when I was little and you heard I wanted to be a magician? You made a magic wand for me out of a wooden dowel that you painted black with white ends. I was so excited when you gave it to me; I thought for sure it had powers." Troy examined Jonathan's face again. Still, there was no movement. "I treasure that memory, and so many others like when you used to lead my brothers and me through the hills in the forest behind your house. We loved those adventures—we thought we were pioneers or something." There was a box of Kleenex on the bed stand. He helped himself to a fistful of tissues and blotted the tears that rolled down his cheeks. "You'd arm each of us with a walking stick and told us to be ready to use it in case we smelled the scent of cucumber because that would mean a copperhead was nearby."

As Troy had grown older it was mostly through his mother that he and Jonathan stayed connected. Troy squirmed with the discomfort that he hadn't put more of his own effort into staying in touch. He wiped his face against the sleeve of his shirt. "Uncle Jonathan, you always believed in me even when I was the most lost. You never gave up on me—not ever. Sometimes that's what we need most, isn't it? We just need someone to see us for who we really are when we've lost the ability to recognize it in ourselves." He thought of what Jules had told him and wondered if he was doing this right? "I know there's a lot I don't know about life, but one thing I'm pretty damn sure of is that life is a precious gift, and we have so many choices when it comes to how we use it. You've been a devoted husband and father, and you're as good-hearted and honest as they come. There's a saying I've heard—something about how people might forget the things you've done or said, but they'll always remember how you made them feel. [8] I'll never forget, Uncle Jonathan. Never."

Troy thought of the guitar in Jules's shop lying unstrung on the workbench when Jules tossed the package of strings next to it and asked him to identify where the true guitar was. Going through all its parts one by one there was no denying that it wasn't contained in any one of them alone. It wasn't even the totality of the collection of all its parts, as the guitar only

---

8 https://quoteinvestigator.com/2014/04/06/they-feel/

came into being in dependence upon each of them, the mind that conceived it, and the mind that perceives it. And now, here was Uncle Jonathan, lying voiceless in the bed—like the guitar without its strings—appearing to perceive nothing. Troy recalled the meditation Jules instructed him to practice, to think about dependent arising in regards to life. So, he began. *Where is Uncle Jonathan, now? I know he's not contained in any one of those parts of limbs, body, senses or even thoughts. Jules said to meditate on the impermanence of life, understanding that birth and death dependently arise through intention, karma, and all the tendencies we bring along through habits of thought. So, basically that means that everyone's birth and death come about in dependence upon our seeds of karmic potential; those seeds of action of body, speech, and mind that we carry with us and that are continually ripening throughout this life and beyond. So, if death is like stepping out of one set of clothes into another, then those clothes will be woven by our karma—virtuous and non-virtuous—and also by all the mental afflictions that are rooted in ignorance and self-grasping, spinning strong threads of anger, pride, and self-centeredness. But even those threads are impermanent. If I can really understand that, then that's wisdom. And wisdom carries the force to eliminate those threads, and to instead weave threads like altruistic compassion, and courage. If I'm understanding all this right, then that's essentially the two wings of merit and wisdom that ultimately eliminate suffering, delivering joy in its place. What I see as Jonathan is not simply that collection of parts. I see them all as Jonathan but isn't it all so much more—or maybe even less—than meets the eye? Each thing changes moment by moment, in constant dependence upon every other thing in the flow of time and space. Like water in a stream, moving over rocks, changing into vapor, into clouds, and then to rain, snow, or ice. Only, instead of water, it's consciousness that moves through different forms dependent on its karma.*

He let his mind rest in this awareness of dependent arising. It was an experience of vast openness, and a profound feeling of bliss where all that existed seemed to be perfect, peaceful, and joyful. He dedicated this perfect moment of peace to Uncle Jonathan, and to all beings everywhere.

He heard Rita and Michelle enter the room accompanied by the nurse.

"I'm just going to check his vitals and moisten his mouth," the nurse said.

Jonathan's breathing had become slower with long pauses between his breaths. The nurse gently turned him onto his side, telling him what she was doing and explaining that he would be more comfortable in this position.

Michelle came to take his hand in hers, "Daddy—Rita, Troy and I are all here with you now." She bent to rest her head against his shoulder. "I love you. I love you with all my heart." She cried, "I'm going to miss you so much." She reached for the tissues, weeping into several she'd pulled from the box. "I'll be okay though, Dad. I promise." Making an effort to laugh she said, "You know better than anyone that I'm stubborn and strong, so you don't need to worry about me." She gently stroked the thin wisps of hair back from his forehead, smoothing them over the top of his head. "I have your love and you have mine. We will carry that with us forever."

Rita and Troy both stood beside Michelle, their hands resting on her back.

As Jonathan breathed, gurgling sounds came from the back of his throat. The nurse used a moist towel to gently wipe his mouth and lips. And then, something changed. In the same way you can feel someone enter or leave a room, there was a distinct sense of departure. His body, now empty of life, lay motionless without even the hint of breath. The whole room fell silent and numb. Michelle looked at the nurse, searching her face for an explanation for what had just happened.

"He's gone," she said softly.

Troy reflected on the teaching he had received from Jules and saw the experience of Jonathan's death through the eyes of wisdom—the power of ripening merit that allows for the transformation of sadness and grief into bliss and joy. He silently imagined sending that bliss directly to Jonathan as a gift; a gift that he could take with him as he moved toward his new set of clothes.

~

Yet the suffering
Involved in my awakening will have a limit;
It is like the suffering of having an incision made
In order to remove and destroy greater pain.
VII. 22

The service had been simple. An intimate group of friends came from nearby towns, and afterwards people shared stories of Jonathan, a man who was well loved and admired. Maggie had come for the service too, bringing clothes that Rita and Troy had asked her to get from their house. And for Troy, the world somehow seemed a little more right—no, maybe a lot more right—when she arrived.

Rita helped Michelle sort through some of Jonathan's things and encouraged her to take her time. "Grieving is a process that can't be packed away," she explained. "You're actually pretty fortunate because there's no timeframe you have to finish this within. I found that by handling some of my parents' things there were little surprises, and in many ways going through everything nurtured memories that felt very comforting. Those memories will mean more and more to you as time goes on."

Troy could appreciate how for Michelle, just touching some of her parents' belongings could be comforting. But he could also see how they clearly wouldn't cause the same feelings to arise for himself or for someone who had no personal connection with Uncle Jonathan. Because the quality of emptiness is present in any object and every person, the same feelings and associations can't possibly be present for everyone across the board. Even so, Troy was happy that

Michelle had these objects to give her comfort along with her fond memories.

~

The evening before they left for home, Rita, Troy, and Maggie accompanied Michelle to the river that ran through the town where Jonathan had lived. It was the scene of many stories he had told from his childhood about fishing with his friends, building rafts, and searching to find old arrowheads. He had told Michelle that when the time came, this was where he wanted his ashes scattered. He said this river would carry him within the fullness of its banks to stroke the earth, and to hold the light of the sun, moon, and stars beneath an ever-turning sky. And so, with hearts overflowing with both love and grief, they wished him a good journey, and then carefully and slowly poured his ashes into the water. Troy silently added a special wish and dedication that Jonathan's future will be one of happiness.

The following morning while Maggie and Rita were talking outside on the patio, Michelle asked Troy to come with her into her father's room.

"There's something I want you to have," she said. "Please, sit down."

She opened the dresser drawer, took out a small blue box and handed it to Troy.

"Open it," she said.

Troy lifted the cover.

"It's platinum," she said. "And those diamonds are an old-fashioned cut; I don't remember the specifics. It belonged to my mother, of course. And there's no one besides me to inherit it. It would be like keeping it in the family if you have it. I've recently had it cleaned and its setting checked. You might not be ready for this, but when and if you are, whether it's Maggie or someone else, it could be a very special engagement ring for the right girl. Having said that, I think Maggie would love the setting and this very sweet scrolling on the band. But you could always keep the diamond and have the setting changed if you'd like."

"Are you sure about this, Michelle?" Troy asked, carefully holding the open box in his hands.

"Of course, I'm sure Troy. Don't think for a minute that I haven't given this a lot of thought."

"Thank you," he said. "And yeah, it will be Maggie—that is if she'll say 'yes.'"

"Well, don't rush, honey," Michelle laughed. "Just because I'm giving it to you now doesn't mean it needs to land on anyone's finger right away. Take your time. You'll know when the time's right."

"Sounds like good advice. Thank you."

"Have you had any coffee yet?" she asked.

"No. But I'd love some."

"I'll go start a fresh pot," she said. "Why don't you find a safe place to keep that ring before anyone sees it and ruins the surprise." She hugged Troy, "Don't forget, no pressure, but I do think Maggie's delightful."

"That she is," Troy said.

~

Having patience, I should develop enthusiasm;
For Awakening will dwell only in those who exert themselves.
Just as there is no movement without wind,
So merit does not occur without enthusiasm.
VII. 1

The following week Troy sat with Jules in the studio. He explained that with the curve balls of his mother's move and the trips to see Uncle Jonathan, what he had expected to be a wide-open summer hadn't gone quite as he'd hoped. And now, in the last days of August he had to turn his attention back toward school. He didn't resent the curve balls, but was disappointed that he hadn't accomplished more of what he'd set out to do.

"Well, Troy, you're not in nirvana yet," Jules said. "This is the way it goes in the world of cyclic existence. In case you've lost track, let me remind you," he said with a laugh, "we're living in samsara, a world of impermanence with a wealth of opportunities to experience suffering including the fact that as a result of our birth we'll also die.

"When it comes to the people we love, normally, most of us can't help but feel deeply attached, and so when we lose them, that loss can literally feel like it's ripping away a vital part of ourselves. So of course, even if you're studying and practicing as you've been and have the wherewithal to observe things from a certain philosophical angle, you're still of this world and sometimes you just have to roll up your sleeves and cope with the world as it is. Having said that, because you've tasted the medicine that the dharma offers you, learn to take these worldly conditions and use them to propel yourself along the path. You do this by meeting them with compassion and wisdom and the intention to benefit others. So please, recall the compassionate way you've helped your mom, your uncle and his daughter, and rejoice in having done that.

"Every bit of what you've done has been an excellent way for you to practice and deepen your understanding of all you've been learning. In the process, you are learning that, instead of clinging and grasping onto those we love, we can be beautifully devoted and even selflessly dedicated to their happiness.

"You know by now that the biggest obstacle in the path is not something like helping your mother move or tending to someone you love who is dying. The biggest obstacle on the path is the ignorance of self-grasping, the root mental affliction—you can think of it as the mother ship of all the other mental afflictions we've talked about, and the one that causes the most intense suffering. Understanding this and meeting life with the altruistic intention to benefit others, infused with wisdom, can give us the necessary courage and enthusiasm to persevere in our effort to eliminate ignorance and all other mental afflictions. If we do this with the wisdom that understands dependent arising and that recognizes the spaciousness we live within, then when we eventually release ourselves from the affliction of self-grasping, a main result is a kind of joy that truly is like some kind of precious jewel, a jewel that money cannot buy."

Jules was circling the kernel of understanding Troy needed to help unravel the uncomfortable feeling he had been struggling with—the sense that he was living a dual life, like a commuter between two worlds. One that was of his daily life of work, Maggie, and all the day-to-day requirements of survival, and the other was the journey he had begun through his dharma study and practice.

"So, let's say I want a job—a job where I can earn a decent income," Troy said. "And let's say that, um, maybe I want to be married one day, and who knows, maybe even have a family. Can I still do all this and have a strong practice?"

"Well, I'm not sure exactly what you have in mind in terms of 'all this.' You can absolutely have a good practice and live a life like you describe. But, you're certainly not going to be able to do it like a monastic would, if that's what you're after. Someone who takes the vows of a monk or a nun carves out a life that is free of things that the rest of us have to contend with, renouncing every aspect of samsara and devoting him or herself entirely to a very dedicated study, practice, and way of life. It's a personal choice, Troy. We often hear about vows of renunciation that monastics take and imagine some kind of banishment into an austere, dry, lifeless life. But that's not the case. What's really being renounced is everything that brings suffering. So, renunciation is what allows those who take the vows to fully enter the path, make progress on, and to complete the path to total enlightenment in a very specific way. A monastic life, that was specifically designed by the Buddha.

"To be clear, not everyone has to become a monastic in order to reach enlightenment, as there are many methods or paths that the Buddha taught us to reach this goal. You don't have to shave your head and put on robes in order to be a dedicated dharma practitioner—these things are symbolic in the way a wedding band is symbolic of wedding vows. True renunciation is something that takes place in the mind. And this includes things like reducing, and ultimately eliminating the mental afflictions and negative emotions that come about through things like hatred and aversion, or any selfish desire that we experience in response to things that come through our senses. It comes also by observing your mind in order to guard against the ten non-virtuous actions of mind, body, and speech. In other words, observe your mind vigilantly to protect yourself from ever causing harm to any living being because remember, if you're renouncing suffering then your renunciation includes the suffering of others. And as I was just saying, if you can do all this, you'll find yourself in a state of incredible peace and joy. And when your mind is in such a state, you'll be naturally moved to actions like altruistic generosity, loving kindness, and compassion—like it would never dawn on you to be engaged in anything but. Just as you brought your practice into all you've been doing this summer you can bring it into everything you encounter in life. With the right understanding of things such as impermanence and dependent arising, your choices on all fronts will be informed by wisdom; your actions of body, speech, and mind, and your relationships with others will be rooted in compassion and honesty; and the work you engage in will be work that in no way brings harm to another being."

Troy stood and began to pace within an imaginary boundary he had constructed in the space of a yard or two on the floor. He thought about the engagement ring he wanted to offer Maggie. He thought about the fact that he still hadn't even figured out exactly what he would do to support the life he envisioned for himself; a life he hoped Maggie would want to share with him. Then he stopped pacing and looked at Jules whose dark and gentle eyes watched him like a sculptor seeing the un-carved shape within the stone.

"I've been married and had four children," Jules said. "My wife has always been interested in archaeology and now, since the children are grown, she's been enjoying the freedom of being able to go on extended trips to participate in digs as a volunteer. Right now she's in Peru helping at some Incan sites. Before she retired, she was a schoolteacher and so her schedule worked well with our four children's school schedules. And me—well, you know what I do," he opened his arms, presenting his entire shop as evidence.

"Personally, I like a quiet lifestyle and enjoy a degree of solitude. But generally, I like people; I like good food, I like having lights in my house for reading, and I definitely prefer having heat and running water to not. So, I guess you can easily observe that I'm attached to being comfortable, which boils down to the fact that I still have a strong case of self-grasping, although ultimately, that's determined by what's arising in the mind. What gratitude do I have for having these comforts of life? Does that gratitude generate true appreciation for this precious human life? Do I realize the only reason I have this human life is due to good karma? And the best way for any one of us to use this fortunate life with all its comforts is to fill our activities in daily life with dharma practice—a practice that will help us put an end to suffering—not just our own suffering, but for others too. That's true compassion.

"Whether it's on the meditation cushion or in all our normal activities of life, it starts with vigilant mindfulness of these fundamental principles, which are all part of the steps on the path to enlightenment. So, if I'm appreciative of these things that make my life easier and more comfortable, if I understand the interdependence of how it is they're available to me, and if I carry a strong degree of mindfulness through my days that holds an awareness of their impermanence, then they can actually help to energize my practice.

"If I cause no harm through my work, and instead do it with the intention to benefit others, then I'm bringing joy to my customers and for that I'm grateful. Again, this is something that energizes my practice.

"I'll go on retreats now and then for maybe a week or two at a time. I haven't sought out a cave, but I carve out a little space in my home, turn off the phone and dive into study and meditation in a specifically prescribed and more focused way than my ordinary daily life permits."

"It all sounds good, Jules," Troy said. "And I can see that you've actually done everything that you've just described. And I also think I can do something similar, but I feel like such an idiot because I still haven't figured out what I'm going to do when I finish school."

"Come with me," Jules said as he stood to cross the studio and waited by the open door for Troy. They walked up the slope past the house to where the grass met the woods, and zigzagged around a thorny patch of wild, black raspberries. Jules stopped to pick a few berries that tumbled easily into his hand and offered some to Troy. Then, pointing to the silver birch that was growing a few yards away, "Notice how that tree's growing. See how its roots are draped like an octopus' arms around that large rock? They reach into the earth, held strong not merely by their own force but by a strong netting of fibers woven of fungal filaments that intertwine cooperatively with an unfathomable network of other underground organisms." He looked up to admire the expansive green canopy of branches and leaves that moved gently in the August breeze within a hazy blue sky. "Trees really do seem to connect multiple worlds, don't they? They extend from the dark depths beneath the ground to stand on the earth and dance in the sky." He nudged a stone, rolling it with the toe of his boot along the path. "This tree has inspired me over and over again, Troy. It reminds me that with my roots deep in the wisdom of the dharma I can overcome obstacles, just as this tree has done with that boulder—in fact, it looks as if it's actually used that rock to be part of its strength. It makes me think about how I, too, can turn any obstacle into my path. And, I know it sounds trite, but when I see how tall it's grown, it reminds me that the sky is the limit. Set your intention, Troy. You might not know the exact, specific thing you'll do for your livelihood, but begin to set your parameters now. Informed by the dharma, they'll guide you by working like coordinates on a map. We can set our intention to grow, not as a separate but as an interactive and interdependent part of life including every kind of being that surrounds us. And with that understanding, your unwavering intention will be to benefit others. It's the not-so-secret but often overlooked intention that provides the fuel, or 'karmic potential' for a joyful and peaceful life."

Just like a farmer's field needs to be cleared and well prepared before planting, the mind also needs to be prepared. Although Troy had heard Jules say similar things in one way or another before, this time his words felt tailor-made. Everything Troy had spent time learning and meditating on up to this point prepared his mind, tilling the field and sowing the seeds so to speak, to actually move his understanding beyond the intellectual and conceptual into one that thoroughly engaged his heart. And now, determination and clarity eclipsed all doubt and hesitation, and he could feel the confident, vibrant force of something he knew must be the joyous effort Jules, Abe, and Mrs. Sternau had each talked about.

"I think I got it," Troy said. "I can work with this. I'm pretty sure I'll never see a tree in quite the same way again." He laughed, "And I can't believe I'm about to say this, but seeing everything as dependent arising, moment-by-moment, I'm actually pumped to dive into school."

Jules smiled, "I think I know the feeling." He glanced at the tree and then back to Troy, "Then, it seems safe to say that you know what to do."

"Umm, you know what, Jules? I know things can always change, but for the moment I'd say I do."

"Once you've deeply experienced something in your mind, even if something knocks you off kilter now and then, you always know what's involved to refresh those coordinates in your mind." Jules laughed, "Like a sailor lost at sea, even in the dark of night they have the stars to go by. Celestial navigation is one of those reliable, old-time things that's always available once you understand how it works. The dharma's not so different. We study it, we learn to understand it, begin to apply it and there you go...you're guided well on your way with a very reliable support system."

"Yeah," Troy agreed, "and staying with that metaphor, I know I'm the one that's got to raise my sails and work with the wind."

"You got that right! And that's the joyous effort. Can you taste the salt air and the freedom of where it can take you?"

Troy closed his eyes and thought for a moment. "Yeah, I believe I can."

~

First of all, I should examine well what is to be done,
To see whether I can pursue it or cannot undertake it.
(If I am unable,) it is best to leave it,
But once I have started I must not withdraw.
VII. 47

Troy woke to the sound of rain, a rain that planned to stay for several days and turn the summer green even greener. The carpeting inside felt damp as he walked barefoot, carrying a mug of coffee back to his room, and prepared to settle onto his cushion. He considered whether or not it's appropriate to sip coffee in between segments of his meditation and then decided that the important thing was that he showed up to practice, and if the coffee helped him get there—well then, so be it. And as Jules had taught him, he was grateful to have the coffee as an aid to his practice.

Since he didn't have the flexibility to rest his knees comfortably against the floor he supported them with pillows, and then followed the guidance he had learned from Grace months earlier. He sat with his spine straight, the back of his right hand nesting within the palm of his left, thumbs touching, and his wrists resting against his thighs. Next was the step of taking refuge which he did by bringing to mind the Buddha with the perfected qualities of wisdom and compassion; the dharma, Buddha's flawless teachings and ultimately the direct experience of seeing all things as empty; and the sangha—those who have achieved higher levels of realizations through the dharma and that provide support through their example and guidance. Troy understood that his mind was the place where the results of meditation take root, and so for anything to be fully integrated into his life his mind must be stable and strong—not unlike the underground fibers that secured the silver birch's roots. So, whether he could picture these objects of refuge in living color or only think about them conceptually, the important part was knowing their qualities and recognizing their infallibility with the same confidence that a sailor regards the guiding stars of the night sky.

He turned his attention to his breath; he felt it enter softly through his nose and followed it through the center of his body. When thoughts interrupted his attention, tugging it away to one thing or another, he'd gently pull it back. Once his mind was calm and still, he rested it in this state for a while.

Next, with his mind focused, he reviewed the practice to cultivate equanimity. He thought about the endless living beings, the humans, animals, insects, and down to the tiniest life forms that he could only barely imagine. Considering that everyone shares the same basic needs for food, happiness, good health, and love, he brought to mind the meditation Jules had taught him while leveling the frets on the guitar in the studio. Just as there should be no highs or lows between the frets in order for the guitar to produce its best quality of tone and timbre, there should be a leveling of attachment or aversion in how we experience all other beings.[9] He imagined a scene of endless beings and allowed this feeling of compassion to expand as far as the universe extends, radiating to each one of them. He settled into that space as if his mind were simply a giant ocean of love and compassion—equanimity toward all sentient beings—and felt a distinct sense of peace and calm dissolve all other thoughts as he let his mind rest there.

Time passed in the unnoticed way it often does when you're thoroughly absorbed in something, until a flock of crows began to caw from the trees beyond his door. They too became objects of his compassion. He finished his meditation by dedicating the merit he had accumulated to purifying his negative karma and

---

9 In equanimity practice, this can only be brought about through meditation on how all living beings only wish to not suffer and to instead experience joy and happiness. And how, through recognizing the opportunity that exists in the teachings of the Buddha to end all suffering, not only for oneself but for all others, one takes on the wish to do so. That starts by leveling off the extreme emotions of feeling attachment or aversion to some sentient beings, and instead, bringing all of them to mind with an absence of such extremes, motivated by clearly seeing their suffering and wanting to actively end their suffering. This is true compassion. John Cerullo, Consulting Editor

eliminating his mental afflictions so he could actively experience equanimity and strive to cultivate the qualities of a bodhisattva so that even as an ordinary person he could live his life fully present and dedicated to the benefit of all beings.

Before leaving his cushion, he brought to mind the image of the silver birch that Jules had shown him, and determined that he would do his best to remain rooted in this dharma practice as his day went on. Over the past several days of considering how he could integrate his practice fully and wholly into his daily life, there was an important decision he had made. There were just a few pieces to put into place first.

Troy took his phone from his dresser to call Maggie. No answer. He sent her a text, "Busy today? Let's go to NYC."

While he waited for her to respond, he picked up his guitar and started playing scales. It had been too long since he had actually practiced the guitar; he felt the neglect in his fingers and heard it in his sloppiness. He reached to turn on the metronome and began again, this time a little more slowly. He ran through a series of scales and then moved on to sequences of arpeggios in patterns of minor and major chords. Finally, the phone rang.

"Hey. What's going on in the city?" Maggie asked.

"I don't know; it's raining. It seems like a good day for a museum."

"Seriously? I'd love it. But, do you even like museums?"

"I don't know, Mags. Maybe. But I'm pretty sure you do; they're loaded with paintings."

"Well, yeah, of course. I'd love it. Sure, let's go."

"Do you know which museum you want to go to?"

"That's a tough choice. Let me give it some thought."

"Okay. I'm looking at the train schedule. If we leave in about half an hour, we can catch one that'll get us into the city by noon."

"Perfect. I'll be ready."

~

Without indulging in despondency, I should gather
the supports (for enthusiasm)
And earnestly take control of myself.
(Then by seeing) the equality between self and others,
I should practice exchanging self for others.
VII. 16

The train had already begun to roll from the station before Troy spotted a pair of open seats at the end of the car. As they settled into their seats, he lightly shook the water from his umbrella and tucked it into his backpack.

"So, did you decide on a museum?" he asked.

"Yeah, I did. I think we should go to the Museum of Modern Art. And if it turns out you enjoy that, then another day we'll check out The Metropolitan Museum of Art."

"Sounds good," he said. "I'd actually like that. A little culture never hurts anyone!"

"Truly? You mean that?" Maggie asked.

"Of course I do."

"Well, we could visit each of these museums every day for a year and still not have seen everything that's there to be seen."

"That's crazy," Troy said. "It's overwhelming how much there is to see and know. I wonder which is better—to know a lot about a little or a little about a lot?"

"I don't know, but when you think about it, none of us—no matter how intelligent or educated—truly knows more than just a little about a lot."

"Huh?"

"Well, think about it. Think how much art is in just one of those museums and the many centuries and cultures each exhibit covers. And that's just inside one building. I think people who think they know a lot about a lot are probably just ignorant to how much exists that's yet to be known."

Troy laughed, "Mags, I thought the dharma was hard to follow, but sometimes you come out with things that are every bit as confusing."

She smiled and said, "Well then, I guess I'm in good company."

"Are you hungry?" Troy asked. "There's a vegetarian restaurant I think you'd like. We can go there before we head over to the museum. We've got plenty of time."

"Sure, let's go."

When the train arrived at Grand Central they threaded their way through the crowds of people to where they descended a steep flight of stairs to the subway below, and joined a crowd of others waiting for the next train to come. A duo on cello and violin played a piece by Bach; their notes blending like woven silk in the underground acoustics. Troy pulled a couple of dollars from his pocket and added them to the money the musicians had collected in the open violin case in front of them. One of the things Troy loved about New York City took on additional meaning for him after hearing Jules talk about the way trees inhabit three worlds. Here, life pulsed on all levels; the endless streams of people in the below-ground level of the subways, those walking and driving on the streets, and countless others that were stacked story after story in the enormously tall buildings that fill the city. Each person's history being played out in moments as they tick through time, the joyful and the broken, the healthy and the sick, the wealthy and the poor, the angry, the bitter, and the loving. Troy felt an un-summoned wave of compassion fill his heart that carried a simple wish, a wish that each one of these people would be met with happiness and peace.

They barely squeezed themselves to fit in the train before the doors slid closed behind them, all the passengers looking someplace where their eyes seemed not to truly see. Standing so close together they offered the only space they could by portraying the sense they're not really there.

The car emptied and filled and emptied and filled again several times before Troy announced the next stop was theirs. They climbed the stairs, and traded the sounds of hissing and clanking train engines for traffic, honking horns, and sirens. Troy opened the umbrella and they walked together beneath it, dodging puddles as they crossed streets for the last few blocks to the restaurant.

~

As a result of virtue, I shall dwell in the spacious,
fragrant and cool heart of a lotus flower,
My radiance will be nourished by the food of the
Conqueror's sweet speech,
My glorious form will spring from a lotus unfolded
by the Mighty One's light,
And, as a Bodhisattva, I shall abide in the presence of
the Conquerors.
VII. 44

The rain had stopped by the time they finished lunch so they walked the remaining blocks to the museum. Taxis raced past, spraying streams of dirty rainwater in their wake and splashing the legs of the less fleet-footed pedestrians. Scents from pretzel and hotdog carts mingled with exhaust; it was a world glistening in light.

Once inside the museum they paid their admission, and Maggie studied the pamphlet of the museum's floor plan and list of galleries.

"Ah, here's the place we should begin. Before we look at anything else I want you to see one of my favorite post impressionistic paintings—maybe even one of my favorite paintings altogether."

"Okay," Troy said. "I don't think you've ever told me you have a favorite painting." He reached to feel for the small box zipped in the inside pocket of his backpack, and took a deep breath to calm the nervousness that made his heart feel like it was churning instead of beating.

"I probably haven't mentioned it before," she said.

They climbed the stairs, and wound their way through galleries and exhibits into a large room partitioned into smaller spaces where paintings could be more intimately experienced. Maggie led him around one of the partitions and stopped.

"Here it is, Troy," she said. "Van Gogh's 'Starry Night.'"

Troy took in the textured layers of swirling colors, the spiraling starlight, and the tall tree in the foreground that connected Earth to the stars. This was perfect. It was celestial navigation on canvas, bridging an entire past directly to this moment. He slipped his backpack slowly from his shoulder and pulled the zipper open to where he had tucked the jeweler's box.

"I can't believe I'm standing here so very close to this painting," Maggie said, leaning as close to it as she could without being scolded by one of the guards. "It's like some part of Van Gogh is literally present right here, like he poured some part of himself into the paint."

All the uncertainties and doubt that Troy had struggled with disappeared; his mind was clear. There was room in his life and in his heart where both his dharma practice and a life with Maggie could coexist.

"Come closer so you can see," Maggie tugged Troy's arm. "If you look close you can notice the way he applied the paints to make even a night sky immensely colorful. Can you see where he left little streaks of the canvas unpainted?"

"It's beautiful, Mags," Troy said. "And, by the way, so are you."

"That's sweet of you to say considering I'm still a bit of a rainy mess. But, thanks." She looked at Troy and saw that his eyes were moist with tears.

"What's the matter?" she asked. "Are you okay?"

"I've been thinking about something for a while. I love you Mags. You bring out the best in me and I want to always be there for you; to do my best to fill your life with love and joy." He offered the box to

Maggie in his cupped hands. "Um, I never thought I'd actually say these words ever to anyone, but I'm asking you if you'll marry me?"

A handful of visitors in the gallery turned their attention from the art to discretely watch the scene that was unfolding in front of the Starry Night.

"I don't know what to say, Troy; I love you with all my heart. And I can promise you my honest devotion." She let out a deep breath and turned away from the painting on the wall, eyeing the Exit sign over the door. "I don't ever want to be married, Troy. I watched my mother let her life be derailed by marriage and I will never allow that to happen in my own. To me, marriage and all its finality under the guise of some contrived sense of eternity is the kiss of death." Maggie reached her hand to hold Troy's, "I will love, cherish and honor you, Troy, but please don't ask me for marriage. I hope it doesn't fly in the face of your dharma teachings, but I don't believe in happily-ever-afters."

Troy felt the sting of disappointment and hurt as he noticed the people who had been watching turn their backs to face the paintings again. His face reddened and burned as he tightly held the closed box with the ring inside his fist. A familiar grief clenched his jaw. Without looking at Maggie, Troy walked to a nearby bench in the gallery where he slumped onto the seat, and let his backpack drop to the floor. Again, he practically heard Mrs. Sternau's words as crisply as if she were right there with him: "*when you're truly awake, every moment is an opportunity to practice.*" With every mental affliction Jules had identified now poised to strike, he had no doubt this was an opportunity to practice. The many hours he'd spent reflecting and meditating on things he'd been learning quickly delivered two powerful words like medicine to his mind: Impermanence and Interdependence. Marriage is not the essence of life; it has absolutely no capacity of its own to deliver lasting happiness. Happiness is the true essence of life, and every opportunity to practice is an opportunity to reveal the clarity that actually does deliver a lasting happiness.

Like water on fire, these initial thoughts began to lighten the sorrow and hurt. Now Troy could begin checking all the boxes of the Four Noble Truths: Was there suffering? Yes, plain as day. Were there causes of suffering? He distinctly felt two of the three poisons: attachment and ignorance. And even without hatred, he could feel the threat of anger, the source being his self-grasping. What about cessation of suffering? Only by applying the wisdom of everything he'd been learning. As he'd learned from leveling the fret board, this would happen when there were no highs and lows between attachment and aversion, and as a result of filing away mental afflictions by recognizing the absurdity of grasping something that only exists like a reflection of the moon in water. What about a path? Yes, in fact the path is very active and definitely not one of passively wishing for things to be different. It's the two wings of merit and wisdom. Wisdom: the opposite of and antidote to ignorance. Recognizing the true nature of how things exist, dependently arising from causes and conditions. Merit: compassion that actively seeks to benefit others. Troy's heartfelt intention had been for Maggie's happiness as well as his own, but clearly, he'd miscalculated and this wasn't going as he'd anticipated. Inching his way out from his own pain, and trying to see things from her perspective, it wasn't hard to understand where Maggie was coming from. He had seen his own mother's life derailed by marriage too. Maggie wasn't wrong; believing marriage could wave a wand of happiness over them like a Disney animation is naïve and futile. Happiness has its own set of causes and conditions. He recalled a passage he had read in one of his books at home, "my happiness depends on your happiness[10]..." The simplicity and the truth of this passage in turn reminded him of something Jules said, *the biggest obstacle on the path is self-grasping,* and *instead of clinging and grasping onto those we love we can be beautifully devoted and even selflessly dedicated to their happiness*. He didn't need to be married to Maggie in order to do this.

Maggie tentatively approached the bench, and lowered herself gently onto the seat next to Troy. They sat quietly for several minutes within the murmur of other visitors' conversations and slow-moving footsteps that took them from one painting to another. Then, Troy took the ring from inside the box and held it toward Maggie saying, "I am giving you this ring only as a symbol of our love. There are absolutely no strings attached. Will you accept it?"

"I will," she said. "And I do."

10 Geshe Lobsang Dhargey

(It will be) so, if I do not forsake the Bodhisattvas' way of life.
Why should someone like myself, who has been born in the human race,
Not attain Awakening, since I am able to recognize
What is beneficial and what is of harm?
VII. 19

Acknowledgments

This book has been written with my highest respect and gratitude for the generations of teachers who have made great sacrifices in their own lives to preserve the Buddhist teachings. Among these great teachers is His Holiness the XIV Dalai Lama. When the Chinese invaded Tibet in 1959, he lost his home and country. Fleeing for their survival and for their freedom, he and thousands of other Tibetans fled Tibet, risking their lives on the dangerous journey over the Himalayas where they were warmly welcomed by the people of India. While the risks to the Tibetan people in Tibet still exist, the world has benefitted tremendously from the teachings, leadership, and perfect example that His Holiness has consistently demonstrated of a bodhisattva—an enlightened being whose existence is dedicated solely for the benefit of all beings. It is without a doubt my greatest honor that His Holiness the Dalai Lama has written the foreword for this book.

There are insufficient words to express the depth of my gratitude to my immediate teachers from Do Ngak Kunphen Ling (DNKL) in Redding, Connecticut: Guymed Khensur Rinpoche Lobsang Jampa, Tenzin

Samten (Sengtul Rinpoche,) Geshe Lobsang Dhargey, Geshe Ngawang Kalsang, Geshe Ian Tashi, Venerable Lobsang Sherab, Venerable Lobsang Nyima, Venerable Lobsang Tendrol, Venerable Losang Donyo, and Ernst Nogaise (Phuntsok.) It is through their kindness, wisdom, knowledge, patience, and generosity that the path of the Bodhisattva is made clear.

I am fortunate to have received teachings from Guymed Khensur Rinpoche Ngawang Jordan, Sera Mey's current Abbot Geshe Tashi Tsering, Jangtse Rinpoche, and Tongkhor Rinpoche. These extraordinary teachers visited DNKL on their travels from Sera Mey Monastery in India and remain close in my heart.

There have been many other teachers and translators who have visited and taught at DNKL, enriching, and shedding light on teachings for those of us who strive to integrate the profound Buddhist view into our daily lives. I know I'm not alone in my deep appreciation of their generosity.

I will never forget master luthier, Paul Neri's warmth and generosity when he welcomed my son, Daniel, and me to visit his workshop in Clinton, Connecticut. He gave us an overview of a luthier's work which enabled me to write about the various techniques Jules and Troy employed in this book. I am also extremely appreciative of the time Paul spent reviewing the luthier's portions of my manuscript, and to offer editorial corrections where needed.

I want to thank my mother-in-law, Mary Quinn O'Hagan Caravella, whose love and joy for life is always an inspiration. Mary worked nights as a nurse while she raised her four children, and continued her work through her early years as a grandmother and frequent babysitter for her six grandchildren. Mary walked me through the likely concerns, and the care that would be given to this book's character, Uncle Jonathan, during his hospitalization.

Another Caravella I want to express my gratitude to is George Caravella, my former husband and devoted father to our children, Geoffrey and Daniel. Beyond our divorce, George has been an enthusiastic support to my music and to my writing over the years. The end of a marriage is never easy, but once the storms pass, love is love. It may change form, yet the enduring family and love shared for our children, and now our grandchildren, is something we celebrate together.

Huge thanks to my daughter-in-law, Sara Caravella who works in New York City. When I was writing about Maggie and Troy's walk from the restaurant to MOMA, she gave me her account of what it's like to walk in the city after a heavy rain. Equally huge thanks to Eliza Bethany and Judith Lambertson who answered questions I had about painting for some of Maggie's segments in the story.

Writing about Buddhist dharma is a subject that I strive to be very careful to accurately represent. In writing this book as well as the previous three, I feel extraordinarily fortunate to have had very knowledgeable people I could turn to for help in clarifying my understanding of specific dharma teachings. As I prepared to begin, Guymed Khensur Rinpoche Lobsang Jampa, with the kind help of Geshe Ian Tashi as translator, answered questions I had about the Perfection of Joyous Effort. Geshe Lobsang Dhargey has been available over and over and over again with unwavering patience and generosity throughout my writing of this book and the others, and has cumulatively spent countless hours talking through the points that I needed to understand clearly before I could write about them. Venerable Lobsong Sherab spoke with me at length, helping to clarify the meaning of renunciation for monastics as well as for laypeople, and also provided other editorial suggestions. John Cerullo, as consulting editor on this book and as publisher for the previous three, has also spent an abundant amount of time in conversation with me, reviewing the book's content, making suggestions, and bringing my attention to areas that needed further explanation. As the manuscript was close to completion, I asked a friend and dharma teacher, Lorne Ladner, PhD, if he would read through the manuscript and double check the text for dharma accuracy. His attention and insights were helpful beyond measure. With the help of all these people, I am hopeful that readers will find in these pages an experiential touchstone to the ancient and wise teachings of the Buddhist dharma. If there are any mistakes in the presentation of the dharma, I want to be very clear that they are my own.

Without someone to manage the final edits, layout and design, and to oversee the process of printing, there could be no book. I have enormous gratitude to Clare Cerullo for her sensitive, artistic, and skillful work on this book, and for the three previous books in this series. I have been able to rely on Clare with confidence, knowing that she shares the vision of what we hope this series of books will offer to readers. And for this reason, I have been able to trust her to treat each book with love and care.

There have been some people that have gone the extra mile for me, and whose love, support and active efforts to help have been the wind in my sails when I needed it most. Gina Brandt at Brandt Advertising, Quinn Caravella, Pattie Copenhaver, Anita Donofrio, Gus Ford, David Kittay, Gary Lefkowith, Joanne McCall, Publicist, Jennifer Richards at Over the River Public Relations, and Robin Stancliff. Writing is an endeavor that requires a great deal of solitude, and often feels quite isolating. There have been many times during this process when each one of these people has made something happen at just the right time, giving me the encouragement I needed to keep the "joyous effort" in motion.

And to more of my family and friends whose love, support, and comic relief keeps my heart full: Tricia Broadbent, Mary Alice Buton, Joan Candee, Anya Caravella, Laura Caravella, Gloria Cosgrove, Jeanne Dankowski, Laura Del Valle, Suzanne DuBois, Nancy Ettele, Linda Fiske, Jeff Fookson, Billy Frolick, Liz Goldstone, Jampa Gyeltsen, Don and Kathy Hallock, Ron Henry, Alice and Steve Hutchinson at Byrd's Books in Bethel, CT, Emily Johnson, Abbe Levin, Gelek Lodo, Victor Lozinak, Lisa Mason, Bob Minton, Bernadette Napolitano, Barney Nelson, Dianne O'Neil, Ngawang Phuntsok, Kirt Pruyn, Greg Raymond, Bruce Relkin, Barbara Pease Renner, Eleanor Roche, Tina Roese, Dr.

Harvey and Diane Ruben, Bill Ryan, John Simpson, Lisa Austin Smith, Stephanie Spinner, Sharon Stancliff, Glenn and Kaori Kawataki Sullivan, Jack Sullivan, Louisa Yap, and Karen Romano Young.

Of course, at the foundation of so very much is my mother, Rosamond Patricia, born and raised on the Indonesian island of Java, and my father Philip Leon, born and raised in Japan who met on a blind date while college students in Boston. Not only did their unique backgrounds draw them together, but also carried an essence of the eastern cultures where they were raised and which I believe primed me for my immediate attraction to the Buddhist philosophical view and path. An extraordinarily important person in my life; someone who was my absolute rock through some very painful years during my adolescence and early adulthood was my great-aunt Gertrude. She had overcome many challenges in her own life, and as a result was able to share her unconditional love and wisdom with me until her death, just six weeks shy of her 100th birthday. Even today, after she has been gone for nearly thirty years, she remains a loving and strengthening presence in my heart. For my sons, Geoffrey and Daniel, I am consistently thankful for their love and support, for the way they light my life and are always an inspiration for me in everything I do. And for the little "bumper crop," a.k.a. my grandchildren, Morgan and Augie... just when you think the love that fills your heart can't possibly expand any further, these little ones enter your life and fill it with more love, and the magic and joy that small children bring with them.